Realities of the
Dreaming Mind

Realities of the
Dreaming
Mind

SWAMI SIVANANDA RADHA

Timeless Books
publishers of timeless wisdom
1994

TIMELESS BOOKS
PO Box 3543
Spokane, WA 99220-3543
(509) 838-6652

In Canada: Timeless Books, Box 9, Kootenay Bay, BC V0B 1X0
- (604) 227-9224

In England: Timeless Books, 7 Roper Rd., Canterbury, Kent CT2 7EH
- (0227) 768813

Printed in the United States of America

Cover illustration and interior design by Deborah Pohorski
Interior illustrations by Margaret White
Editor: Julie McKay

Library of Congress Cataloging-in-Publication Data:
    Radha, Swami Sivananda 1911-
        Realities of the Dreaming Mind/Swami Sivananda Radha.
           p. cm.
        Includes bibliographical references and index.
        ISBN 0-931454-68-9 (hardcover)
        ISBN 0-931454-69-7 (paper)
        1. Dreams—Religious aspects   2. Self-realization—
        Religious aspects   3. Yoga I. Title
    BL 65.D67S58   1994
    294.5′446—dc20

                        94-16766
                           CIP

Published by
Timeless Books
publishers of timeless wisdom

Dedication

This book is dedicated to all the Gurus I have met, but especially to Swami Sivananda of Rishikesh and to Hugh Lynn Cayce. It was Hugh Lynn, on his visit to our very simple ashram in the early 1960's, who first inspired me to look for the divine messages in my dreams and eventually led me to pursue my study of Dream Yoga.

Contents

Acknowledgments

I do not have enough words to give the recognition which is deserved by the many people who offered their labors of love in creating this book. For her patience and persistence in working with me as my main editor I wish to extend my thanks to Julie McKay. For the design of the interior and the cover I wish to thank Deborah Pohorski, and for the illustrations my gratitude goes to Margaret White. I would also like to thank Jayne Boys for her valuable suggestions, Joyce Ansell and Karin Lenman for their advice and copy editing, and Diane Conway and Norman MacKenzie for their research assistance. All of these people are seekers after the same goal—Liberation. May this book assist them on their paths. It would not have been possible to publish this book without the finances generated by the fundraising efforts of Russell Oughtred, Susan Oughtred, Donna Pace, Lynn Fairey, Janet Gaston, Jeannie Guillet, Elizabeth MacLeod, and Pat Carty. I am also grateful for the individual contributions made by others, including Janet Brown, Frances Becker, Mary Ruth Green, Deborah Brillstein, Sylvie Lalonde, Francine Joly de Lotbinière, Cynthia Poole, Sharon Wobker, and Ramona Mitchell.

I wish to extend special thanks to the publisher for having the courage to publish books that are not just for supermarket shelves but are for those who seek the Most High.

A Word from the Author

FOR MANY YEARS I was reluctant to make this material available to a larger circle than my immediate disciples. My dreams were often the most intimate and guiding experiences of my life—experiences that helped me to realize the Guru within. But now that I am near the end of my life, I felt I could bring myself to relate these experiences to others in the hope that they, too, will dive deeply within and discover the inner kingdom of God. It is also my hope that this book will contribute to an understanding that the great Truth, the true Light, the real Essence in all religions is the same, even though expressed in different symbols. Once we understand this, we have no need to convert others or to change our own paths. We only need to intensify what is already there.

Foreword

*D*REAM RESEARCH has become one of the most hotly contested battle-grounds for opposing viewpoints in the behavioral and social sciences, demonstrating the conflicting perspectives in regard to the so-called "mind/body problem." Many neuroscientists believe that mental phenomena are merely reflections of more basic and fundamental physical processes, and that science's perceptions of physical objects are more real, more valid, and hence more trustworthy than its perceptions of people's mental activity. They are saying, in effect, that studies of the "body" are scientifically respectable while studies of the "mind" are not. However, many other investigators take the perspective that a rigorously conducted psychological experiment or phenomenological study can be every bit as scientific as a well-controlled piece of research on neuronal activity.

These psychologists insist that human behavior cannot and should not be conceptualized solely in biophysical terms. Human activity needs to be understood in terms of its purpose, intentionality, and psychological significance. Psychologists need to look for motives and reasons, not just for mechanical causes. In the case of dreams, neuroscientists have made great contributions in describing how dreaming occurs, but many of them stop there and assume that the evoked images and memories are derived randomly and lack substantial meaning. They do not consider the possibility that Rapid Eye Movement (REM) sleep produces the necessary and sufficient conditions for dreams to occur without, however, determining their form and content.

Perhaps the mind's brain sets the stage, but it is the brain's mind that writes the script.

Swami Radha's approach to dreams is congruent with this perspective. Her "Dream Yoga" is an avenue to self-understanding, inner development, and spiritual liberation. Swami Radha knows from experience that dreams can be used to cultivate awareness, acquire wisdom, and enhance intuition. She rejects the Freudian model of the unconscious that sees it merely as a repository of repressed desires and unacceptable thoughts. Like the Swiss psychiatrist, Carl Jung, she understands that the unconscious is a treasure trove of latent potentials, unused capacities, and undeveloped creativity. Swami Radha shows through her own dreams how dream work can be used as a spiritual discipline and how the very process of dreaming constantly confronts the dreamer with such questions as What is real? What is illusion? Do some dreams disclose memories of past lives? Do some dreams provide directions for living this life more fully? Rather than supplying her readers with easy answers, she encourages them to unravel these mysteries themselves.

In *Realities of the Dreaming Mind,* Swami Radha describes a "Guru within" that is often unacknowledged during the distractions of the day. At night, however, this inner Guru has less competition for the statements it wants to make. By pointing out the dreamer's own destructive thoughts and images that limit growth and discernment, it can free the dreamer from accepting unwarranted criticisms and judgments from others, and allow the person to develop an opening to what Swami Radha calls "Higher Consciousness." She outlines a basic procedure to assist this process: suggesting that one's dreams will be remembered, writing down the dreams, working with them, composing a personal "dream symbol dictionary," and putting the resulting insights to work. Her method of dream interpretation includes recalling the events of the day that may have led up to the dream, writing down an immediate impression of the dream's meaning, recording the words and images that seem to be the most important, then making associations to each of these key items, and putting the resulting message together. She also tells her readers how they can collaborate with other dreamers in group dream work.

The timing of Swami Radha's book could not be better. It coincides with what many people have called the "grassroots dream movement" in the United States, Canada, and several other countries. Groups of dreamers are gathering together to work on their own dreams, realizing that psychotherapists do not have all the answers and that dream groups offer an opportunity to explore the social and cultural dimensions of dreaming, as well as the personal meanings.

These groups are community-based and often meet in schools, libraries, or people's homes. There are artists' dream groups, women's dream groups, and dream groups for recovering alcoholics. There are dream groups held in churches, synagogues, ashrams, and other places of worship and contemplation. There are dream groups that focus on the creative aspects of the dream, others that search for the spiritual side of dreams, and still others that emphasize personal growth and development. Many community-based dream groups cut across socio-economic boundaries as well as those of gender, race, and age. Dreams are one of the few human activities that allow for either a homogeneous or heterogeneous mix of people to participate. Swami Radha's book is an excellent resource for members of these assemblages because it gives dreamers the tools to appreciate and understand their own dream narratives and images.

Finally, this book urges dreamers to define, discover, and describe their own reality. The ancient philosopher Marcus Aurelius wrote, "Those who do not know what the world is, do not know where they are." In recent decades, humanity's world views have become more and more diverse until conventional realities seem to have been torn and shattered beyond repair. Western world views, whether religious or secular, have held that there is one absolute and permanent reality, and that this can be known and comprehended by revelation or by reason. Eastern world views have been more flexible, acknowledging the always illusory, repeatedly oscillating, and ever-shifting nature of reality—and realizing the shortcomings of both revelation and reason as exclusive paths to the truth. Eastern philosophy has emphasized the utility of intuition, awareness, and inner discipline in humankind's attempts to unfold the paradoxes of existence, unravel the enigmas of being, and attain union with the Divine Light within.

Dream reality and waking reality share more similarities than differences. In the *Yogavasistha,* a sacred Hindu text, dreaming sleep is described as an opportunity for human beings to create as the gods create, by emitting images. Just as divine forces "dreamed" the universe into existence, humans constantly "dream" their own worlds into existence. And just as the pictures painted by the Divine Artist enfold a more profound reality, dream images enfold deeper meanings if dreamers would take the time to find them.

While the West has urged people to look "out there" for their supernatural or material actualities, the East has advised an inner search, a quest that depends on neither dogmatic scriptures or material technology, thus a journey that is available to everyone. *Realities of the Dreaming Mind* brings this venerable tradition into the contemporary world, a world that ignores dreams and visions at its risk. Swami Radha's book places dream work directly in the collection of yogic disciplines that continue to satisfy those men and women who value spiritual exploration and the search for meaning.

Stanley Krippner, Ph.D.
Professor of Psychology
Saybrook Institute
San Francisco, California

I

THE FOUNDATION:
WORKING WITH DREAMS

Introduction: My Approach

OR MANY YEARS dreams have had a
deep impact on my mind and have influenced my major decisions and activities.
By combining the yogic teachings and
practices with my understanding of symbolism, I have
studied and worked with dreams in order to open a
dialogue with my unconscious mind. My goal has been
to attain knowledge of the Divine, leading to Self-Realization and Liberation.

Dream Yoga, as I call this approach, is a way to get
in touch with your Higher Self, or the forces of the soul,
through involvement and analysis of your dreams. To
practice Dream Yoga you need a teacher who has per-

sonal experience in investigating dreams and applying their wisdom in daily life. Therefore in this book I will base my presentation on my personal experiences. I only teach what I have tried out in my own life, on my own mind. I do not experiment with other people's minds. Increasing quality in life and expanding awareness are the only approaches that I have to offer. How much do you want to know about yourself? The increase of awareness is up to each individual.

Working with your dreams will help you to develop intuition, and it can eventually open the doors to the Divine within. But first you have to accept yourself precisely as you are, with your feet firmly on the ground of your present existence. You do not, however, have to remain a victim of your mind, letting negative thoughts and images play over and over like a broken record. Yoga is a process of dehypnotizing and waking up. As you bring awareness to your dreams and discover your daydreams and illusions, you may also find that you are capable of greater control of the mind than you had imagined.

This is a path of gradual unfoldment. It is not possible to practice any branch of yoga without practicing awareness. We are getting to know ourselves. In fact what we are doing is creating a map of the mind. While the map is not the thing itself, it will help us understand where we are starting from and where the mind can travel in the process of thinking, imagining, and dreaming. There is a constant interplay of forces between the body, the mind, the emotions, the unconscious, other minds around us, memory, and our own illusions. There are so many influences at play in the mind that we need a clear way to investigate it. Dreams can help us. We learn how the mind functions while we think we are asleep, and we learn how we can influence the mind while we are apparently awake. In Dream Yoga we want to bring together the conscious and the unconscious with a desire to gain mastery over the mind and to give power to the true Light within.

As you work with your dreams, you will become aware of your own "soul" or "Higher Self" or "inner Light." Your soul, which is the gateway to the Most High, will obtain the wisdom that you need and give it to you, provided you get in touch with that power in yourself.

~

Before going further I will clarify some of the terms I use and what I mean by them. In the West we have many concepts of the unconscious. I will use the familiar term "the unconscious" in a specific way. I will refer to the unconscious not only as a purely psychological function of our own individual, personal life, but as a much larger part within the Cosmos (which is a big word that might sound exaggerated but is not).

The unconscious, in some Western schools of thought at least, is considered to have no discrimination and to be like a storage cellar for hidden enemies that try to make us miserable by shooting at us and producing adverse effects from their dark corners. From the Eastern point of view, that definition is unacceptable. I like to think of the unconscious as a big ocean in which many things have their life, a life unknown to the conscious mind and inaccessible to a strictly psychological understanding. Through the unconscious, the past can be illuminated and brought to the surface, at least to the extent to which our courage and ability allow this. Often we are limited by set ideas, concepts, and strong beliefs and convictions which have served their purpose in daily life but keep us within self-created prisons.

What we are "unconscious of" is what we are not aware of. The Eastern meaning of the unconscious is, essentially, "not being fully aware." When we practice yoga, we try to expand awareness in order to achieve control over that which is generally considered impossible to control, and to attain direct knowledge of what is considered unknowable. We try to attain that knowledge by delving into the unknown, expanding experiences, and fearlessly pushing accepted limitations further and further away.

There is no doubt that many things we do and think arise from the level of the unconscious. But if we expand the meaning of the unconscious to encompass more than our personal life—to include the three worlds of existence (the physical world, the mental world, and the celestial world)—we can conclude that everything we do not know is part of the unconscious and needs to be discovered. That which we are unconscious of includes *Kundalini energy*, our latent creative potential.[1] Kundalini energy can be compared to the soul in the Christian teachings, because in the same way that Kundalini is latent, your soul is really unknown. You have to awaken to the fact that there *is* a soul and that you can contact it; or from the perspective of Kundalini, the soul has to be freed from the imposed sleep of the mind.

---

[1] For more on Kundalini, see Swami Sivananda Radha, *Kundalini Yoga for the West* (Spokane, Wash.: Timeless Books, 1978).

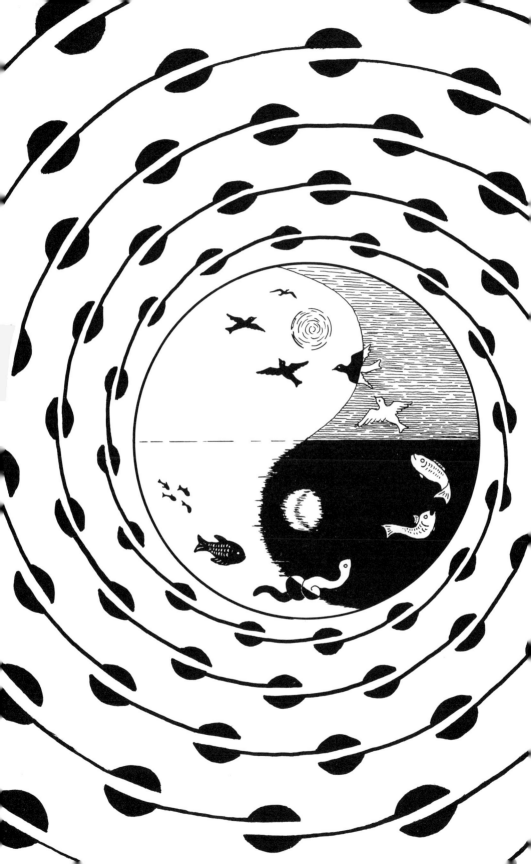

If we do use the word "soul," the soul must be understood as being perfect rather than being capable of error. If you can think of the soul as perfect, as the divine spark within, then the concept can be a link between Western philosophy and Eastern symbolism. The sleeping or latent energy called Kundalini is equivalent to the latent energy that we call the soul. And your soul self *knows*. If we can contact the soul through dreams, we will be in touch with this powerful creative spiritual force.

~

In Part One of this book I present the basic method of working with dreams. In Part Two, I explore the questions of the interrelationship of the conscious and unconscious, reality, illusion, creativity, and the powers of the mind. In Part Three, I give instructions in the practices of Dream Yoga and some examples of spiritual dreams, or what I call "dream experiences."

Although the book is entitled *Realities of the Dreaming Mind*, I do not attempt to define "reality" for the reader. Instead I give examples of my own dreams and experiences and ask you to question for yourself: What is real? What is illusion? What is dream? You are given the freedom to explore and to find your own way, accepting and defining reality according to your understanding. If I spelled out my ideas too precisely, you might imagine that you now *know* what reality is and would not think for yourself.

In the same way, when I discuss past lives and even give some examples of my own dreams in this area, I do not make a definite statement that past lives are a reality. Investigate for yourself. Your view will depend on your vantage point—whether you are in the valley, or half-way up the mountain, or on top of the mountain, or behind it. Also your viewpoint will change according to your state of development. How many times have you rejected something that you later came to embrace? Our perspectives shift as we develop.

As you approach your own dreams, you should start with the basic method, being willing to face whatever the unconscious brings up, and applying your understanding in your life situation. As you work with your dreams, you may start to ask questions about the mind that produces dreams. What is the knower that can communicate these messages you need to hear? Why can you not hear the messages with the conscious mind? This leads to questions about perception in daily life. How much is daily life influenced by faulty perceptions and illusion? What is the difference between reality and dream? Finally, if your desire for the Divine is intense, you will want to maintain contact with the Light at all times, and life itself may take on a dreamlike quality. You may receive dreams that can lead you to higher levels of mind and greater sources of knowledge.

When you are in touch with the Light within—the Light being symbolic for the Divine—then dreams can indeed lead you to a greater reality.

1

The Value of Dreams

RE WE LIVING in one world—the world in which we walk with our feet? Or do we live in another world—a world of thought and dream? Which is real? When does life become a reality and when is it just another dream? Who are you? Why are you here? Where do you come from? Where do you think you will go?

By reflecting and working intensively on your dreams you will find answers to these questions, and you will see how much more there is to discover. The objective of the yogic approach to dreams is to contact the Divine within—what the Eastern teachings call the *Guru* (spiritual teacher) within or the Higher Self, and what Jesus calls the kingdom of God within[1] or your own soul.

The yogic method of working with dreams emphasizes independence and stresses understanding ourselves as individuals. Our dreams are our own creations, and as we study them we learn our personal language of the unconscious. Making our own discoveries is a very joyful process and gives us the courage and strength to go on. By finding answers within, we gain self-confidence. We do not depend on someone else to interpret our aches and pains, which can be seen in a thousand different ways. There can be no generalization about symbols because we each develop our own symbolic language.

We can look at how, in our own lives, we have grown up to understand and use language. We should not think that the process we began as children has ended. Learning becomes more cultivated, more refined, more expanded. We learn to use our tools more skillfully. If you become aware of how you use words, you may discover why in the East the power of speech is called the *devi* or goddess.

Our unconscious will provide us with a great deal of information if we give it a chance. But we have to use a methodical approach because we do not really know how our unconscious speaks. In the conscious mind we have become fantastic acrobats. We can argue and rationalize everything. The unconscious comes and knocks on the door and says, "Look, I'm here. Remember me." We need to recognize how the unconscious is struggling to attract our attention: "Please listen to

---

[1] ". . . for, behold, the kingdom of God is within you." Luke 17:21

me!" We need to learn to see and to listen to this inner wisdom, because if we do not, we will find ourselves in dramatic or traumatic situations in life.

It is strange that we think we know each other and we think we know ourselves very well, but when it comes to the language of the unconscious, we are really quite ignorant. We have to study it as we would a foreign language.

Ask yourself, "Do I want to study my own symbolism? Am I really interested in myself?" Clarify your motivation. Why do you want to study your dreams? What do you hope to gain? This questioning creates a willingness to learn and a goal to work toward.

There is a well-known story about a little girl who walks until she comes to a crossroads. She asks herself, "Now which is the right way for me to go? I don't really know." She looks and looks but cannot make up her mind. Suddenly she sees a hut. She knocks on the door and an old witch comes out. The little girl asks, "Can you tell me which is the right way to go?"

The witch responds by asking, "What is your destination?"

The little girl says, "I don't know."

"Then," says the witch, "it doesn't matter which road you take."

You must tell the witch of your unconscious where you want to go. When you have clarified your ideals and know what kind of person you want to be, your dreams and dream experiences will tell you how to get there. Your dreams can suggest the next step, and even how to take the step. The unconscious will tell you your potential, but if you do not follow through and apply this guidance, your potential will not be realized.

A young woman living at the ashram[2] said that her spiritual teacher had come in her dreams and told her she should stay at the ashram. He even gave her specific instructions to follow. But one day she met a nice young man, and suddenly she had a whole series of completely different dreams whose message was, "This is the man of your life. You should follow him."

I asked, "Which dreams do you think are true? Did you manufacture the first dreams? You were convinced at the time that they were a kind of higher guidance, but now you tell me that your new dreams are giving you a very different message."

Was the unconscious playing tricks on her? I think not. The first dreams had revealed her spiritual potential. She chose to ignore her potential by ignoring the previous dreams and by interpreting the new messages in a way that satisfied her emotional desires. In this case the man was with her for only a year and then left. The unconscious will show us our potential, but if we do not follow through and make use of it, the unconscious will offer whatever is next best, which is usually the generally accepted way of living.

You have a divine birthright, but if you do not claim it, the only one to blame is yourself. You cannot say that you are not given the opportunity. You are in the exact circumstances you should be in, until you make a greater effort to grow. You can make your aim the highest goal—

---

[2] An ashram is a spiritual center that provides a setting for those pursuing awareness. The ashram I started is called Yasodhara Ashram and is located in British Columbia, Canada.

the Divine within. Find out for yourself if there is anything to it, but you need to be determined to know for your own sake.

Dreams can keep you going and keep you nourished. They also provide a positive outlet for self-interest and self-expression. Our inherent selfishness can be used in a most beneficial way—to get to know ourselves. You will find that the many images in dreams give you both positive and negative information about who you are and where you are in your development. Your dreams can tell you what nobody else can. Twenty people can give you twenty different opinions about yourself, so where does that leave you? If you sincerely want to develop, how do you know whether what they are saying is just their projection or is a message you should work with? How can you know if a person is being used as a divine channel? Your Guru within will make it clear through a dream, as if to say, "Look. Here is a major problem. You must work on it." Dreams can help you become independent of the criticism or judgment of others. They have a powerful influence and can really change your life if you are willing to listen.

During the day your mind is too active to hear the Guru within. You go into mental gymnastics to justify your actions, to do what the emotions pressure and direct and coax and sometimes coerce you into doing. You are driven into action by emotions, so you are not free. When you go to sleep, the busy mind fades out and higher thoughts can come in to treat the aches and pains of your problems by showing them to you in another way. Dreams make us aware of things that, when we are too busy, too attracted by brightness and colors of life, we do not "see."

We often say we want to be a channel for something higher; if so, we have to be a channel that is well-scrubbed. Otherwise it is like opening an old water tap: out comes all the debris—little bits of rust and dirt and silt. Dreams have a marvelous way of showing us the dirt that is in our water pipes, how to identify it, and how to remove it. Some things may not be all that visible, but dreams will help us to recognize them. We will always have this invaluable guidance from within ourselves.

We are so proud of logic and intellect and yet we create the most ridiculous problems for ourselves in our lives. That is what the unconscious shows us in a kind, slow, gentle way, giving us the message little by little, step-by-step, so that we can see it without the little ego being completely crushed. Dreams can make us aware in a very loving, beautiful way. Sometimes they also shock us or shake us awake, but only when we do not listen or when we just do not want to get the message.

If we want to understand dreams, we have to see what stuff they are made of. What is their fabric, their texture? It can be very fine, very gross, very beautiful. And it is from the situations in which we are most receptive in our waking state that the unconscious takes the material to deliver its message, to help us to help ourselves.

By looking into our own dreams and keeping careful records, we can learn a great deal about ourselves on a purely psychological level. It is good to begin on that level. Later we may receive specific instructions from

our dreams. Finally, we might slowly develop the opening to Higher Consciousness.

When you have erected the tabernacle in your own heart, the secret place of worship, you begin to build Jacob's Ladder, or the steps that are needed to approach the Higher Self from your good foundation. At this point, when you have awakened intuitive understanding and finer feelings, you need to tread very gently and carefully and not rush in like an elephant, stomping and crushing everything. You simply notice and ask, "What does this mean? Why did this suddenly come to my mind?"

I suggest that you first learn to work with your dreams using the method I will give you—write your dreams down, analyze them, create your own dream symbol dictionary, and investigate how your unconscious uses words and symbols to get a message across. Studying your dreams and expanding your understanding of the symbolism and the imagery of your unconscious can open a whole beautiful new world.

Recognizing the Most High in yourself is like entering a cathedral, where all your senses are touched. You can explore the Cathedral of Consciousness into which you are born by listening to your dreams. The dream voice will guide you: "Come along. Open this door. See, here is another room you can enter. Go down the hallway. Here are more doors. This area looks a little dark, but next time you will know how to find the light."

2

The Method

T HE METHOD OF investigating dreams that will be presented here is a safe way to open the doors to the unconscious and will give clear-cut results in time. It will take time because dreams at first seem very confusing. Until you learn the language of your unconscious and until you gain the courage to look at the naked truth, your Higher Self is very gentle and will cover up the truth a little. Your dreams will have greater clarity as you learn the procedure for understanding them and as you grow in strength and willingness to look at the problems that they bring up.

The unconscious is very kind. It does not sail in and say, "You bad person! Change that!" The unconscious is most gracious and gives you the material in the most appropriate manner—sometimes in a very polite, indirect way and sometimes very directly. You will see how the unconscious becomes your most reliable, loyal, and true teacher. Then one day when you speak about the God within or the Guru within, you will really know what you are talking about. It will no longer be a theory or fiction.

How do you go about working with dreams?

RECALL

Recalling your dreams accurately is the first task. To help with recall, you must first create a deep desire to remember.

Just before falling asleep, address yourself by your first name and give yourself the suggestion, "As soon as I wake up, I will remember my dream. I will remember my dream." Making this suggestion twice helps it penetrate the polarity of the mind.

Before you turn off the light, have all the essentials next to your bed—paper and pencil and maybe a flashlight. At the top of your paper, put the word *Dream*, and the date, with day, month, and year. Alternatively, if you use a tape recorder, have the tape in and ready to go. Train yourself to wake up without an alarm, or if you set an alarm, lower its volume.

In the morning when you wake up, immediately write down your dream. If you cannot remember a dream, you must still take action. Before you set even one foot out of bed, take your paper and write down the feeling that you woke up with, or the first thought that comes to mind. In other words, do not let the lazy part of your mind have control. Insist on obedience and you will see that your mind can be very obedient. Writing this first thought indicates the intensity you have demanded of yourself. If your first thought is, "Oh, I didn't seem to have a dream," write this down along with the accompanying feelings. Even recording the fact that you do not feel good about it may help you to pursue the memory of the next dream.

If after three weeks you still do not remember a dream, you have to look at yourself honestly. Sometimes we pull down the blinds because there is something we do not want to know.

DREAM RECORD

Write down your dream just as it is, even if it is short, and even if you have only a few small details. These are always very important. Decide that you will be absolutely honest and will not make changes to make yourself look better. You will not have the benefits from the dream if you tamper with it. Sign your name to it to assure yourself later that you can honestly stand behind the accuracy of your dream record.

First write the major content of the dream so that you do not lose the overall picture. Then add the details—that the staircase was on the left side of the house, for example, or on the right side, or in the middle. If you can write all the details from the beginning without losing the overview, then do so. Even if you remember only little snippets of dreams, write them down under all circumstances. With willingness you will remember many more details.

If you have a dream that you feel you do not want to record, or if you have a secret fear of others reading your dream, write it down anyway as accurately as you can. Read it over three or four times. Think about it. Work it through. After you have worked it through, destroy it. But do not ignore it. Whatever the dream tells you, face it, otherwise you will collect a lot of skeletons in the closet of your mind. It may comfort you to know that at a later time, when you have grown in understanding and acceptance, you may see something quite different in the same symbolism and dream.

COMMENTARY

Next make a quick commentary. How did you feel when you woke up? Anxious, overjoyed, elated, miserable, fearful, worried, startled, indifferent? This can be just a short description, perhaps only one line, but it may provide a very important clue.

Was your heart beating fast? Were you anxious? Were you making a fist? Were you holding your hand tightly over your face? Had you picked up an object, such as your watch, from the night table? How did you find yourself sleeping? On your left? On your right? On your back? On your stomach?

Write down your feelings as soon as you wake up. If you try to recreate the feelings later, they can quickly take on a new color. If you dream of mountains, you may wake up with an underlying fear that the mountains are obstacles. But later you might look at the dream and convince yourself that mountains are a symbol of aspiration and that you felt good in this dream. Memory is not dependable.

The degree of intensity of a dream—indicated by your feelings when you wake up and by your immediate interpretation—gives you a clue about the dream's importance.

INITIAL INTERPRETATION

What is your initial, or inspired, interpretation of the dream? Write this down, even if you think the interpretation is insufficient, even if you have only an inkling of the message or only one single thought, or even if you think you really have not the faintest clue where to turn. Even if you think, "I don't really know what it means… it's rather confused," this is at least partly what the dream means—confusion. Then go into the details to find out what the confusion is about, and why there is confusion, in what areas, and what has led up to it. The dream, then, is giving you a rather precise answer.

An engineer friend of mine had this dream.

Bridges Over Roofs

The dream setting was a very beautiful shore on a lovely river. Where there should have been walks, gardens, flowers, trees, and bushes, there was instead an ugly industrial area. In the dream the engineer was building a bridge over the river onto the roof of one house and over the roof of another house. The bridge had some very irregular steps— a very steep one then a very curved one, with several steps going down then the next going up.

He said to me, "This dream doesn't make sense."

I asked him, "If someone gave you this project, as an engineer, what would you say?"

"Confused nonsense."

"What in your life deserves that same description?"

The dream itself was not confused but clearly pointed out to him that his present plans were arising from a state of confusion and would lead to nonsensical results.

CONSCIOUS CONCERNS

Make a commentary on what you think led up to this dream. If you keep a daily diary, refer back to the events and thoughts of the preceding day. What was on your mind? This could include certain anxieties, actions, or reactions. Write down the events that took place: My father-in-law visited. My boss called me into his office. I am Protestant, but I went into a Catholic church to have a few quiet minutes for myself. Three times my eyes were attracted to the title of a book.

Maybe you had a bad day. You wanted to sign a contract that did not come about, or you were applying for a job, without success, or you had a dispute with a loved one. Perhaps there was something that seemed insignificant but stayed with you, such as a certain melody that went through your mind all day. Write down these lasting impressions. They are very important. Include whatever you think might affect your dreams—whether it is your food intake, the phase of the moon, or the atmospheric pressure—to find out if they are an influence or not. Note especially the influences which occurred directly before you went to bed such as movies, television, books, last minute conversations, or any spiritual practice before sleep.[1]

Look, too, at the underlying issues in your life. Do you have any particular plans? Are you trying to make a decision? You have to be quite open in your investigation. What is going on in your daily life that could contribute to the dream?

KEY WORDS/SYMBOLS

Write down the "key words," which are the most significant words (including people, objects, actions, settings), in the order in which they appear in the dream. This will help you to find the precise interpretation. It is a somewhat methodical approach, but it will be effective. Then, as if learning a new language, write down what the words mean—not the meaning as it would be defined in the dictionary—but what the words mean to you, even if you think this meaning has nothing to do with the dream.[2]

What does a car mean, a tree, a flower, a key, a pearl, a diamond, a piece of cake, a piece of machinery? What does running mean, driving, jumping, opening, closing, stopping? Sometimes you may select a group of words, and sometimes a single word. I usually recommend that you look at an important phrase both as a unit and as individual words; the meaning becomes clearer through one or the other.

Let us say you dream you are walking down the highway. You go into a house, open a window and look

---

[1] Spiritual practices are described in chapter 23, "Dream Yoga Practices," pages 261-273.

[2] Refer to chapter 3, "An Example," pages 31-39.

out, and see something outside—an animal, a bear. What does a highway mean to you? What does walking mean? What does a house mean? What does walking into a house mean? Do you remember any more details of the dream? What was the house like—small, big, light, dark? Where was the window? Did it have any curtains? No curtains? You opened the window. How did you open the window? Of course, you can only write down what you experienced in the dream. Maybe you came to the window and it opened by itself. Or suddenly—dreams are strange—there is a window open. What does a window mean? What does looking out mean? If you looked out and there was a bear, what does a bear mean? Were there any trees, or bushes, or flowers, or was the landscape bare? Bear among trees. What do trees mean? What kind of trees? Were they dead? Snow-covered? Cherry trees? Apple trees with blossoms? Was the bear running toward you, or was it just standing there looking at you?

I was looking out the window. I. How did you see yourself as *I*? Which *I* is this? *The window.* You might write, "A window is to let in fresh air, a window is to let in light, a window is to look out of, to keep in heat," or anything a window means to you: "It's transparent, keeps the rain out, keeps the snow out, keeps the cold out." Is it the window of the house, or the window of the door of the room? Is it the window of the mind? Ah! At a later point, you might think "window of knowledge." You "saw" something or understood something looking through a window of knowledge. *Was looking out the window. Looking out.* "Looking out from myself, directing my vision through the transparency and thereby

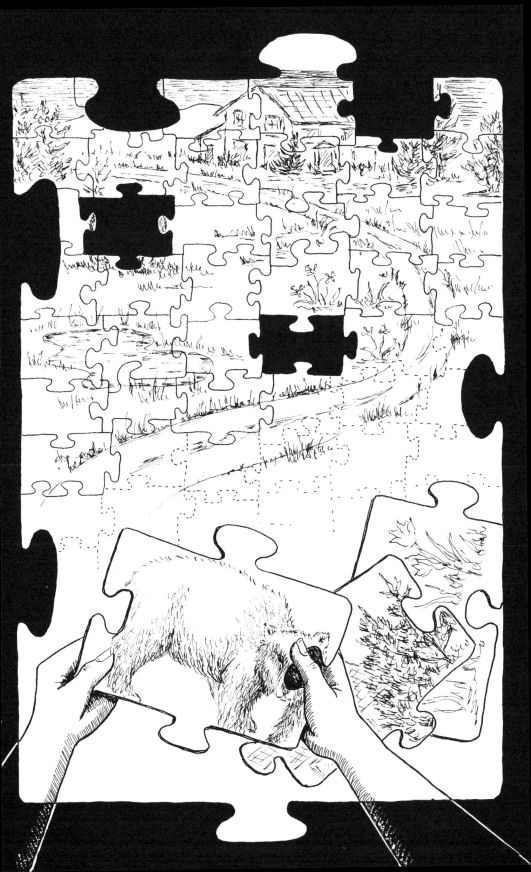

seeing something outside. Taking a different viewpoint, opening a different window to life and looking through." Each symbol will be stepped up as you grow in understanding. What at first looks crazy or nonsensical will become very clear.

INTERPRETATION

Now, with the help of what you have discovered by opening up the dream symbols, you can start to interpret your dream. Go through the dream, key word by key word, then in groups, then in whole sentences, and finally begin to put the message together.

Try to see the dream from different angles. One single dream can be interpreted on sometimes two, three, four different levels. If you put the emphasis on one thing, how does the rest of the dream look? If you put an emphasis on another part of the dream, how does the rest of the dream look? Then look at the whole dream once again. It is like interior design: "What if I put the dining room furniture there and the living room furniture here, and the television in the hall?" You may think it will look just right, but you will only know after you try it and you can see the pieces in relationship to each other. Going through this process is very important.

APPLICATION

Interpreting your dreams and getting their messages is not enough. You can speed up your evolution only if you act on the messages. If you do not act on what you discover, how can it have any effect? Intellectualizing does not take anyone anywhere. You have to apply your understanding in your life.

WORKING IN GROUPS

A dream gives you all the information you need; therefore you can work independently. However, others can deepen your investigative efforts through questioning, and that is why it can be helpful to work in a group.

If you do some group work, you will see more obviously that each person has a very different language of the unconscious. If husband and wife come to the same group, they can see their differences. And as they talk about their dreams, they will see that their differences can be very significant. Are they willing to be friends in spite of the differences? Can they let each other grow in their own freedom or can they not? Insisting on "my way" can prevent growth, but listening and accepting can lead to greater understanding. When people work together on their dreams, a great trust and confidence can be built.

When you go to your dream group, bring a dream that you have already worked with. Always interpret your own dream first, then the group can help you look into other possibilities. If you tell me your dream without interpreting it first, and if I give you a pleasant interpretation of the dream, you will be happy about it. If my interpretation is unpleasant, you may think, "Well, it's *my* dream after all, and I don't see how that can apply." You may accept it temporarily. But even if you do, when I interpret your dream, I can only interpret your dream as if it were my dream and I would get a very different message.

If you have already interpreted your dream, the group can ask, "Could it mean this?" and "Have you looked at this?" or, "From my impressions of you, I would think the dream could mean . . . ." There can be something else to learn from other viewpoints, and at times you may have missed the point, like the woman who thought a dream had proven that her mother was a terrible woman, when really the dream was revealing her own characteristics.

Take the other viewpoints into consideration, but do not depend on them. Another person may be more objective and see something quite obvious that you do not want to look at. However, it is not necessarily so; and it is up to you how far you accept an interpretation from another person. Others can open another window and help you see something, but they cannot demand that you see it, because you are a different individual. Members of the group can give you another angle. But first you have to interpret your own dream, otherwise you can become dependent.

Do your own work quietly by yourself, and when you come together as a group be clear about your purpose. Do not make a social evening out of it. Do the work that is needed in the time given, because none of us knows how much time is left to us. Nobody knows. That is very important to consider. Do it now, not in another lifetime.

When you are in the group, be aware of your own thoughts and feelings and motivations. Analyze the urge to "share." Do not pretend that you want to talk about your dreams if you only want to impress people in order to be accepted. Be honest with yourself and with others.

SUMMARY OF METHOD

DREAM RECORD
>   Write your dream quickly and honestly.

SIGNATURE
>   Put the date on it and your signature underneath.

COMMENTARY
>   Add any details you may have missed. Describe your feelings.

INITIAL INTERPRETATION
>   What is your immediate impression of the dream's meaning?

CONSCIOUS CONCERNS
>   Briefly note events that could have led to the dream.

KEY WORDS/SYMBOLS
>   Select the main words from the dream and write down associations and meanings to you.

INTERPRETATION
>   See how the symbolic meanings fit together to give messages on several levels.

APPLICATION
>   Apply the dream's message to your life.

DREAM GROUP
>   If you find it helpful, you can work with others to get different perspectives.

3

An Example

*T*O ILLUSTRATE HOW this method works and how to explore the many meanings of your dreams, here is an example of one student's dream—first with his interpretation and then with my questions and suggestions for an expanded interpretation.

THE BASEMENT (A STUDENT'S DREAM RECORD)

In the basement, in a corner sitting by an empty fire is an old, gray-haired woman, somebody's mother. Her husband has quietly left her. He gives her plenty of money regularly, but she is entirely alone. We go down in an elevator which then goes horizontally through open base-ments of other buildings and perhaps out into the country.

(signature of dreamer)

COMMENTARY
My feelings after the dream: some compassion for the woman, but only very slight.

CONSCIOUS CONCERNS
I've just completed the three-month course at the ashram. I'm trying to face some unknown obstacles to my develop-ment, in order to take the next step.

INITIAL INTERPRETATION
Something about an attitude change.

KEY WORDS

basement—*is a vital area, a storage area, a packing area, a deeper level*

fire—*warmth, enthusiasm, heat, consuming*

corner—*backed into, not comfortable, out of the swim*

the woman—*intuitive, receptive, nurturing, stoic, emo-tional*

mother—*warm, philosophical, productive, selfless, compassionate*

husband—*reluctant companion, independent, energy source*

money—*energy, resource, and freedom*

elevator—*to change levels, mechanical, no effort, cut off*

horizontal—*level*

buildings—*physical structures, bodies*

country—*natural, free of social implications, change*

THE DREAMER'S INTERPRETATION
My intuitive aspects, now with some maturity and a deeper level, lack fire, enthusiasm; my active side is providing energy, but no support. Mechanically and without effort on my part, I am moving to a lower level than expected through foundations and structures needing completion.

HOW TO EXPAND THE INTERPRETATION

If we look at the dream more closely: not every house has a basement but this one does. Could it symbolize the unconscious? The dreamer is protecting himself. He does not say, "*I* am in the basement sitting in the corner by an empty fire." He says, "In the basement sitting in a corner by an empty fire is a . . ." using the third person to describe the character sitting there. He has to look at which aspect of himself is in that basement. To begin to acknowledge that the old woman relates to himself, he can rephrase the sentence and say, "I am in the basement, sitting by an empty fire," or, "In the basement, I am sitting by an empty fire." That immediately brings it into a personal perspective: "That's where a part of me is—in this vital area, this storage area, this deeper level. Something of me is in contact with the unconscious."

A fire cannot be "empty." Either there is a fire or there is no fire. Even a heap of glowing embers is not empty. If the fire has burned out, there is no fire but only ashes; or if everything is prepared but the fire has yet to be lit, there is no fire. But an "empty fire" must have a specific significance.

Part of the process of going deeper into the meaning of a dream is to ask yourself questions. This dreamer might ask himself, "Is the emptiness really in the fire or is it in the way I perceive it? Is my understanding of the fire empty?" The dreamer's interpretation of the empty fire was a lack of enthusiasm, but could it be more than that? "Here I am in the basement, and here is the fire. What am I going to do next?" Is there ignorance of the purpose of being in the basement and ignorance of the purpose of the fire? It may be that the dreamer has a lot of opinions, misconceptions about life and the purpose of life. He may have accumulated a long string of past experiences that have not been dealt with, which would be much better burned because no profit can be gained from just holding onto them. It is like having stocks in a company that no longer exists—better to burn them than to clutter up the basement with them. That is one possibility.

The other aspect is that if the fire is empty, it is waiting for something to fill it, it is waiting to burn away the old concepts, lack of understanding about the purpose of life. It is like the fire in alchemy in which metal is transformed into gold or the dross is burned away. In Eastern symbolism fire is symbolic of the wisdom that burns away ignorance.

And yes, the dreamer can also kindle more enthusiasm. So the symbolism points to all these aspects at once. "Fire is warmth," he says, "enthusiasm, heat, consuming." The dream may be suggesting that he needs to go into the basement of his own mind and clean out the corners. By lighting a fire he can see what is in the basement, what is hidden in the corners and covered with

spider webs and dust. The dream can convey a message to all of us that we need to see what is in the unconscious and deal with it, removing whatever is unnecessary.

In the corner is an old, gray-haired woman, somebody's mother. The dreamer says, "The corner: is backed into, not comfortable, out of the swim. The woman: intuitive, receptive, nurturing, stoic, staying power, emotions."

The dreamer is keeping this intuitive, receptive part of himself backed into an uncomfortable place rather than making it a part of his life. She is entirely alone. He can ask himself, "How do I cut off my own intuition, receptivity, nurturing qualities, emotions?" The woman also represents "somebody's mother," and "mother" to him, means "warm, philosophical, productive, selfless, compassionate." He should reflect on how he is isolating himself from this very positive aspect. Perhaps he needs to think about his relationship with his own mother, or even his "spiritual mother" or Guru, if he has one. Does the dream reflect back something of his relationship with either?

He can ask himself what image comes to mind when he thinks of "old, gray-haired woman?" Does he reject the aging process and the implication of death? Or does age represent wisdom gained through experience, or perhaps even the soul itself?

Although the dreamer in this case is a man, the old, gray-haired woman could indeed be symbolic of his own soul. If this is the case it would mean that his own soul, the inner wisdom or Light, is neglected and unrecognized. The dream points out that "the husband," which could mean how the dreamer sees himself—active, independent, an energy resource—has quietly left her, perhaps because he got so intrigued with life, business, success, the outer attractions of the world. It suggests that nothing dramatic has happened. He just ignored her—quietly left, instead of giving attention to the soul. He probably nourishes his body very well, perhaps he even follows a special diet, but he does not nourish his soul. He only sends her enough energy to keep her surviving.

The first spiritual marriage is between the male and the female within, the union of reason and intuition.[1] Here the female part of the dreamer is ignored and the male part lives and follows his interests somewhere else. He sends money or energy regularly (out of duty? guilt?), but by his actions he is saying, "Don't bother me. Because if you bother me, I have to look at myself and ask, 'Who am I? Why am I here? Why was I born? Why did I even come into the basement? What are you doing in the corner? And why must I recognize that you are a part of me, and I am part of you?'" He is saying, "You don't need to do anything. Just stay in your corner and be quiet." He gives just enough not to be bothered. Could this represent the attitude that he should do just enough good to smooth over a certain heartlessness or even guilt?

The dreamer will eventually have to accept this feminine part in himself, and when he does, he will be in touch with the wisdom and knowledge which are the powers of the divine feminine.

---

[1] See Radha, *Kundalini,* and Swami Sivananda Radha, *From the Mating Dance to the Cosmic Dance* (Spokane, Wash.: Timeless Books, 1992), for more on the union of the masculine and feminine within.

The next step in the dream is his descent in an elevator. Do you recall what happens when you step into an elevator? You push the right button and wait and let the elevator carry you. However, you have to be sure you push the right button so that the elevator goes up or down to your destination. But this is a peculiar elevator. It goes down, then it goes horizontally. Could this symbolize a linear way of thinking? The elevator, which is used for going up or down to different levels, instead travels on the same level. In the West our way of thinking tends to be rational and linear, influenced by Greek thought and particularly by Aristotle. The horizontal elevator reinforces the idea of linear thinking and indicates again that the dreamer is not in touch with his potential depth. Perhaps he is understanding something superficially.

The dreamer might have misconceptions about spiritual life, perhaps thinking that seeking higher values in life means a life of self-sacrifice and martyrdom. That is absolute nonsense, because in that case there would be very few takers. What we need today are people who want to stay in the world and live a spiritual life—that is, a life in search of higher values. It does not matter how many robes you wear or how many austerities you perform; if you do not live your ideals and help others live theirs in a practical way, it is all theory. Doctrines only create barriers. They separate people of different religions. What really matters is the application of higher values, awareness, and insights. That is what makes a person spiritual.

The other basements are open, so I would suspect that the dreamer is in contact with people who have been quite courageous about looking into their own unconscious. And perhaps the elevator will take the dreamer into the open country toward new horizons. When you can see options in your own life, then life takes on a new meaning, even if initially there is no enthusiasm and the fire is temporarily just burning away, empty, with no apparent purpose. The purpose will be discovered. The dream gives a message as clear as can be.

So what appears to be a very small, almost insignificant dream of only a few lines carries an enormous message, if looked at carefully. This is a beautiful dream.

4

Symbols

*T*HE DREAMING MIND turns the experiences of our daily lives into metaphors and symbols, intertwining several ideas into a single image. It is as if the unconscious takes a heap of loose strands and fibers and creates something different, to which we give a new name—a rope. But a rope is only a rope as long as all the strands are intertwined. If we take it apart, where is the rope? As we "take apart" our dreams by exploring the symbols, we discover that the strands and fibers connect us back to ourselves in a rich, multi-layered way.

Why do we dream in symbols and metaphors? We relate everything to what we have already experienced,

and most of us experience the world around us through our eyes. We are constantly creating images in our minds—it is the process by which the mind thinks, stimulated by emotions through imagination. It is also the way memory functions. The unconscious uses these images to convey its symbolic messages.

Your own dream symbols will carry a different meaning from anybody else's because you are quite a different person from anyone else and have very different life experiences. There may be great similarities in meanings, but they will never be identical, just as there are not even two identical leaves on the same tree. We must recognize our specialness and importance—but in a healthy way, not an egotistical one. We need this healthy sense of importance to sustain the willingness to explore ourselves, which is the path to self-knowledge.

What are the symbols in your dreams, and how should you approach them?

PEOPLE IN YOUR DREAMS

First look at the characters in your dreams as parts of yourself—what I call "personality aspects." Every one of us has a multitude of different personalities that move like actors into the foreground in various situations, and each personality aspect has its own ego.[1] From this perspective, the characteristics of the people in your dreams, whether you like it or not, apply to yourself. If you can accept the criticism that dreams bring to you through

---

[1] For more on personality aspects, see Radha, *Kundalini*, 106-109.

the characters, you have a powerful tool for overcoming your own shortcomings.

The unconscious is very compassionate. It does not zero in and say, "You are that or this." Your unconscious says, "Look, you don't really like this person. Do you know why you don't like her? Because of these characteristics. Now maybe if you look at yourself, you will find that you, too, have those characteristics. You would do very well to look at this despotic father of yours or that crabby little sister." If the dream shows you your bad-tempered friend, Louise, realize that it is not important that Louise is bad-tempered, but that you are, too. And what will you do with your bad temper? The dream is a mirror showing you precisely as you are.

The dream may also reflect your positive qualities and your potential through very inspiring characters. The message may be, "Look, you're not only your mistakes. Here is your kindness, generosity, humor, intelligence."

Working with dream characters is a helpful way to learn that all is one. You may not have all the characteristics that this person has, but you may have some. Then you can see the tremendous interconnection among all beings and understand that you are not really an isolated island.

You might have crowds in your dreams. What is your relationship to the crowds? Do you know where your place is? Are you manipulated by these crowds, or do you remain aware of your individuality and accept responsibility for your actions? The power of other minds plays a role in our lives. We live in a world of billions of minds, with thousands or even millions in the city where we live. We function among hundreds of people, and the dozens that make up our family and those in our immediate surroundings. We have to see how they affect our life. Dreams can reflect these influences.

The peculiarity of dreams is the *I* in them. Who is this *I?* Who is watching, and who is acting? There are different *I's.* When you say, *I see*, or *I think*, or *I live in a cave*, which *I* are you talking about? To which personality aspect does this *I* belong? What does *I* mean? This is the very first step, clarifying the *I*. Where is the *I* located? What or who is it that says *I?* And who knows that *I?*

I am driving. Who is the *I* that drives? Who is in control? What is driving you?

I am stopped. What is the *I* now? Somebody is stopping. It is somebody else who stops you. What is the authority that can exercise its power and make you stop?

I am worried. Who is *I* this time? Who is the *I* that is worried, and what is worrying you?

I do make a very quiet connection. This is a different *I*. *I* do, *I* act, *I* make, *I* am the doer. What happens when there is quiet? What is the connection?

I recognize. A different *I* again. The *I* of recognition. You have not known, then suddenly you are aware.

I am going this way. Who is the *I* that wants to go its own way? What is your way?

Look at the *I's* in the dream as the many aspects of your personality; find out who they are and how they act. Sometimes the *I* can have a double meaning. One person had a very interesting dream that we only deciphered when we finally took the word *eye* (sense organ) for *I* (me). Suddenly the dream became very clear. My only inkling about why the unconscious sometimes uses words in that way is to teach us to be more attentive, to listen more carefully, and to be less hurried. In Old English, "the eye in the wall" was an expression for window. The eye can see through the opening in the wall. The inner eye of wisdom can penetrate any obstacle. Knowledge will penetrate this human house. Which *I* has inner sight?

How will the ego show up in the dream? If it is rather inflated, it may appear as a character who is a bit extravagant, big, fat, fancy, boisterous, or loud. Decide what you want to trim from that extravagant ego.

Once you have understood the dream characters as parts of yourself, you can ask if they also refer to the actual people involved. For example, if in your dream there are people who try to intervene and prevent you from reaching your goal, they might symbolize not just your personality aspects, but those people in your life who say, "Why do you want to be different? Come on, let's have fun. Have another drink." They feel threatened if you are different. If they can keep you from pursuing your goal, they feel justified in their own laziness.

You can also have dreams that refer to your relationship with another person, and other dreams that are actually premonitions or warnings about someone else.[2] However, always look at your dreams first as a personal reflection. Do not jump too quickly to other conclusions.

---

[2] See chapter 10, "Prophetic Dreams," page 107-115

ANIMALS IN YOUR DREAMS

As human beings we often do not recognize our connection with other forms of life. But in our dreams we may find we have many animal symbols. Ancient religions often used animal symbolism, and that is sometimes interpreted to mean that the people worshipped animals. Did they? No, they recognized the animal's particular sharpness or power and used the symbols to express that power. In the same way, gods and goddesses or demons are really personifications of powers. The energy that manifests in a vision of Jesus in a dream can also manifest in the opposite—a monster or murderer. There is a polarity in each of us, the positive and the negative, and we are capable of expressing either. The energy is one, but how we use it is a tremendous responsibility. How do you exercise this power that is really one—that is good, that is bad?

When you have animals in your dreams ask yourself, "What is the characteristic of the animal?" Each will convey an important message to you, showing either a quality that you should strengthen in yourself or one that you should be careful about or get under control. The animal may indicate that you have some strength or ability not yet acknowledged.

You have to find out what each animal means to you. For one person a rat can be a warning that someone is undermining him or her. Someone else may be reminded that the female rat is the most affectionate and caring mother. To one person a dog means faithfulness and loyalty, while to somebody else it means unpredictability and aggressiveness. Another person may associate a dog with having no pride—you can beat a dog and it still comes back.

One person dreamed about a large animal but was not afraid of being attacked because the animal had downcast eyes. Something particular was being implied—with downcast eyes, we cannot look at things straight. It turned out that the problem in this case had to do with sexual self-gratification. The behavior in question was so suppressed in the person's mind, because of conditioning about how sinful such action was, that the dream was saying, "There is no need to fear attack, but there is something that needs to be looked at clearly."

The experiences that every one of us has gone through are still within us and have shaped our lives; these same experiences can also be the tools that help us to interpret our dreams. There can be no general rules for understanding a symbol because each person is unique and influenced by his or her own particular conditioning.

Vehicles in Your Dreams

The car is the vehicle by which we move. I move by using the vehicle of my mind, the vehicle of my intellect—thinking, reasoning. What is the vehicle for consciousness? In old fairy tales the mind was often symbolized by the horse, the camel, or the elephant, depending on the culture. In Europe the horse was as sacred as the cow is in India. In the old mythology, the king or the great knight would ride his horse—his victory vehicle—into Valhalla, the heaven of the ancient

Norse gods. But in modern times the vehicle is often a car, or sometimes a train, a bus, or an airplane.

Look at the vehicles in your dreams. Which vehicles appear? Who is in the driver's seat? What condition are the vehicles in? Do you know where you are going? If you sometimes dream about a little old Volkswagen and at other times a huge black limousine, what does each vehicle imply, and what is the difference between them? What do they say about your mind? If you have a huge transport truck in your dream, what is the cargo of the large truck? Why is a large truck needed? If there is a ferry onto which you drive your car, and you are carried across the water, is this the vehicle that will take you to "the other shore?" Are you going home?

Perhaps you have a train and an airplane in the same dream. What do you associate with train—trains of thought? training? on the right track? or a rigid way of staying on only one track? How does that compare with an airplane that flies in the open skies? What are your feelings about airplanes—fear? enjoyment? surrender? What does an airplane mean in contrast to the train?

SETTING

Where does the dream take place? You are the surveyor of the land of your own mind, which sometimes appears like a tropical rainforest, then a desert; sometimes a meadow full of colorful flowers, then an icy mountain. You see your interior landscapes in the scorching sun and in total darkness. All these different views are important in coming to know and understand yourself.

If you dream you are in the mountains, what are your associations for mountains? Are you at a higher level in yourself? A place of clarity? Perspective? If you see mountains as obstacles, what are the obstacles you are facing? If you find yourself in a river, are you going with the flow or are you struggling against the current of life? You may find yourself in a desert, surrounded by sand dunes, where your eyes have no point to fix upon, and your efforts create mirages; perhaps you feel desperate, desolate, without options, facing nothingness. Sometimes you may dream about being in a courtroom sitting in judgment or feeling judged. At other times you could dream of a church or temple. Does this reflect the need to go inward, to contemplate the purpose of life? Or you might literally find yourself at a crossroads—being at a place where you have to make a decision about your next step.

These are just a few of many possibilities. You can see how the setting of a dream can show you "where you are" in your life or what you need to look into.

WORKING WITH A SYMBOL

Become involved in the symbol. Look at all the possible ideas and write them down, even if you think there is no validity to them. What happens is that when the rational mind has exhausted itself through the outpouring of ideas, intuitive perception can come in—if not immediately, then through another dream.

If you have a dream with a table ask yourself how you use a table and for what. Include the idioms you use—a table to sit at, a place to eat, put a table between us, table a discussion, put all your cards on the table.

Here is an example of questions and suggestions that came up as I guided a person through exploring the symbol *bear* in a dream.

Was there a person in your life when you were young who was like a bear to you, and who still looms large and threatening in your mind?

It may be important to ask, "Who is the bear in the family?" But the bear is not necessarily somebody else. It can also be your own very powerful emotions that compel you to act in a certain way. Is the dream perhaps pointing out that you need to do something about these wild, compulsive emotions?

To some people a bear means strength. Could the bear symbolize your destiny, or a force that has tremendous power over you? Is it the power of karma?

If the bear stirs up a lot of fear in you, look at your fears. Take a piece of paper, fold it in half, and write down on one side all the fears that you can recognize; on the other side write down where you think the fears came from. Some fears may only be the misconceptions of an uncultivated mind and uncultivated emotions, and by looking at them you may be able to let them go.

Make a list of all the bear stories that you can remember, right back to the story of "The Three Bears."

A bear is a very strong and powerful animal, but children also have teddy bears. Did you have a teddy bear, or are you somebody's teddy bear?

What is the life of a bear like—the male bear, the female bear, and what about the life of the cub? If the young bear is pushed up a tree when it is only two years old, is that too soon? Did someone push you into a difficult position? Too soon?

Take time to think deeply about the symbol. If a dream seems very powerful, go back over the preceding three, four, or five dreams to find out what they can add to your understanding, and watch very carefully the dreams that follow.

REFLECTION ON ONE SYMBOL

If you think for a whole week about what one dream symbol could mean, you may find yourself in for a big surprise. By pursuing the meaning of your dreams with this much intensity, amazing new areas can open up. For example, I had this dream of a spider.

The Spider and Her Web

There were two trees, and a spider was weaving a beautiful web at the outer edge of the branches between the trees. It was early morning, and the sun played on the silk. A few little dew drops sparkled like honey drips. But then the spider started pulling the thread back into itself. Apparently it hadn't caught anything to eat or devour, so it decided to go somewhere else. I watched, fascinated, as it pulled in the thread. After all the thread was in, the spider moved somewhere else and started laying out the circumference, one thread first—the web is never perfectly round if you look at it—and started to construct a new web.

I woke up before the web was finished, knowing that I had seen this process in actual life, too. Then I began to reflect on the symbol. What can it possibly mean? Do I spin webs? Is somebody else spinning a web? Who is the spider?

I reflected on it for a week. I started to realize what a terrific lesson the spider taught. It finds a place and releases from itself the material to make a web to catch what nourishes it. It suspends itself in mid-air, until finally the wind blows it to a place where it can hold on. In spiritual life it is the same. Something emerges from us. It is a thin thread. It could break at any moment in the wind of life. From the place where it has fastened the thread and from which it could dangle dangerously, it can get hold of something. From my first meditation I got hold of something in my life. I went to India holding on tightly.[3]

The first four or five points to which the spider joins the web are the points from which it creates its foundation. Then it walks along, and spins out the other threads, and captures flies and moths. We build a spiritual net, and in it we catch inspiration and sublime ideas. They are then ours—they are in our net. Eventually the spider withdraws the silk because it cannot find any more food, so it finds another place, and does the whole thing all over again. When certain practices become mechanical we turn to another practice to continue the search for the spiritual insights that sustain us.

Continued reflection on the spider and its web brought my understanding of the symbol to this next level. Around the time I had the dream, I was leading a class in which we were discussing the energy through which the Cosmic Intelligence creates this whole cos-

---

[3]See Swami Sivananda Radha, *Radha: Diary of a Woman's Search* (Spokane, Wash.: Timeless Books, 1981). I had no background in yoga when during meditation I first met my Guru. Because of the reality of the experience, however, I left everything to go to India to meet him. Naturally I was "holding on tightly."

mic play. I had brought some pictures of Divine Mother Kali, who gives birth to one child at the same time she devours another child, symbolizing the cycles of life. People understood the symbol intellectually, but it did not quite touch them. I was searching for a way to put this complicated philosophical view into a metaphor that would make it much more clear. That is when I had the dream about the spider.

Now I could say, "Look at the divine force as the spider; from that source this whole world is spun out. Think of the Cosmic Energy as the spider's silk, just as fine. And the dew drops are our own planet, and galaxy, and other galaxies. At one point all this energy will be withdrawn back into the Cosmic Intelligence, to be spun out again somewhere else."

Astronomers talk about black holes and think that everything will finally collapse, condensing its energy until it becomes so dense that it will not reflect light anymore. But what is going to happen to the black hole? Will it not at some time begin to expand again and spin out new galaxies, new planets, new asteroids, new stars? The cosmic cycles continue.

So my little dream spider brought a big message.

Do Not Identify With the Symbol

As you work with your dream symbols, I suggest that you do not identify with any of them, animate or inanimate. Although some schools of thought instruct you to identify with every image in a dream, from a spiritual perspective this technique can lead to strengthening concepts that you are trying to loosen. If you dream of a tree, do not try to *become* the tree. A tree cannot move, is deeply rooted, and often has its roots inter-mingled with others, which cannot be distinguished from its own. If you identify with a tree you are rein-forcing a physical attachment to the earth. Instead you can ask yourself, "What does a tree mean to me?" See the many meanings in the symbol until finally the sym-bol itself becomes very flimsy, something you can see through. You can contemplate the energy behind the symbol, but do not identify with the thing itself. If I dream of a dog, I would not identify with the dog be-cause my level of consciousness is different from hers. Objects in a dream—a beautiful crystal bowl, a lovely chandelier—can only convey a message. I do not want to identify with anything but my Higher Self or inner Light.

Identification is a very delicate thing. We are often already confused about it, and it is not advisable to in-crease the confusion by identifying with many different images. If you identify with objects and other people, you will never discover your own divinity. Ask yourself what you want to identify with. Do not even identify with what is dearest and closest to you—your own body. Identify with the source of your true dignity—your Higher Self, or inner Light, your Buddha nature, or your soul. Meditate on what your soul is.

DREAM SYMBOL DICTIONARY

Not only do we gain precious guidance through dreams, but also we can start to see the tremendous range of our own symbolism. Make a copy of each dream's key sym-bols with their many different meanings to you, and at the end of each month put the symbols together alphabetically. If you work with a computer you can do that quite easily. Your willingness to work in detail will bring results. By going through this process you will learn a lot about the functioning of your mind.

Expand the meanings of the symbols as you go on. It is not enough to know what "tree" meant two years ago or even two months ago. The meaning is not necessarily the same now, especially with all your efforts to change; you are not the same so your symbols are not the same. If you go through your dream symbol dictionary, you will find which symbols have already evolved: from the tree in the forest, in the park, in the street, in the garden, to fruit tree, the tree that gives shade, the Bodhi tree of meditation, to the Tree of Life, and the Wishing Tree of the heart center.

As you work with your dreams, clarity may come when you look at the levels of meaning of the symbol. For example, if you write down your associations for the word "water," you might start by thinking: water— to take a shower, to clean, to wash my clothes, to water the plants. But later you think more deeply. The water of life? What sustains me? Water—emotions—rough or calm? Water under the bridge—nonattachment. Water—fountain of youth—memories of old fairy tales. Water of immortality? Water of illusions, the mind— clear or murky? Water to quench my thirst—the thirst for life, for spirit? You may have evolved beyond the first meanings of the symbol long ago. By looking at the different levels, you may enter that intuitive mental space of dusk or dawn.

As you compile the dictionary of your unconscious, you will begin to see how your unconscious uses your own words to communicate important messages. Through your efforts to learn your own language, you will have good, clear insights that gradually make you independent of other people's advice, judgment, or criticism. Your dream symbol dictionary will also show you how you have developed, which can contribute greatly to your self-image. It is like finding treasure in your own backyard.

...

5

Interpreting Dreams

*A*FTER YOU HAVE explored each symbol, take time to reflect on the dream as a whole, seeing it as an entire picture. It is like standing on the roof-top and looking out over the ocean—you have a larger vision than when you are sitting inside the kitchen, where you can only imagine the ocean. Even if you do not recognize the complete message of a dream, by working with it you will be given the inspiration to think. You will gain insights which improve your self-image and help you move toward your goal. If you take the same dream and look at it a year later, you may see twice as much as you see today. But if you make the attempt to try to understand, the Higher Self will not keep you waiting. It will give you the missed messages in another series of dreams, like beads on a string. It will tell you where to go. But the first dream is the first encouragement.

We need to accept whatever emerges from the unconscious—both the positive and the negative. We have to deal with both. The positive and the negative are part of the same unit, like erasing—one hand holds the paper and the other rubs. And you may discover that something may seem negative only because it temporarily inconveniences you, but it may not be negative in itself. Therefore we have to develop discrimination.

Dreams are gentle, but they make us work. The Higher Self sends you the dream in a particular way for a reason. You have to find out the reason. This is why dreams have to be carefully worked with. Write down your first impressions without hesitation, but be very careful about superficial, quick answers. Look for the real message in your dream. Otherwise, you may overlook its importance and miss the help that is immediately available. You may receive the help in six months, a year, or two years, but in the meantime the message could have been extremely helpful and it was not.

The dream does not wave a finger and say, "You bad woman. Here is what you have done. Look—terrible!" The Higher Self is not judgmental. It says, "Better be careful. There is a piece of rock sticking out—you could easily hurt your head." Then the dream leaves it to the dreamer to find out what that piece of rock could be. If you cooperate and work with the dream, you will discover the meaning.

The Higher Self is most kind. It will give you what you ought to know in a way that will hurt you the least. Therefore you become courageous. If you are willing to look at whatever dreams present to you, then you will grow in perception and in the ability to grasp their message. Just as children's stories are embellished and embroidered to catch the children's interest and to hold their attention, dreams will sometimes exaggerate to capture our attention. A very short dream is easily forgotten. If it is too long we may lose the details, but still it may intrigue us.

When we have become very courageous and are able to drop the interference of the ego, we can accept a straightforward message. The unconscious will only give us what we are willing and able to deal with. That is very important to remember. If you ask for your dreams to become short and clear and to the point, they will be—in the proportion to which you grow courageous enough to accept them in the short, direct version. You can have a dream and see in an instant what the message is if you really want to see it. You can come to the point where your Higher Self says, "Now let there be no mistake, this is what it means," right in the dream itself.

I will give you an example from one of my own dreams.

The Five Children

I came into a room and a lady was sitting at a round table with five of her children, having breakfast. The youngest was a baby sitting on the mother's lap banging its spoon. When they had eaten, she sent the four older children off to school. Keeping the baby in her lap, she turned to me

*and said, "You are going to remember your dream. This
dream is important. Don't forget it. I will interpret it for you
right now: The five children are your five senses. Four of
them are going to school and being trained, but the fifth
you are neglecting—hearing. Hear the inner voice. Listen
with the third ear."*

The dream gave me marvelous instructions. It told
me precisely what I had to do. At the time I was indeed
working on the development of my senses, but somehow it had never occurred to me that we could become
sensitive enough to develop "a third ear," a sensitivity
that can hear the tears held back in the voice—the very
finest perception of this sense.

About a week after the dream I was almost literally
pushed into the development of workshops, which have
since become the foundation for teaching at the ashram.
Several psychologists had offered to do a course on group
work, and the program had been publicized for almost
a year. The night before they were to arrive they called
to say that they were stuck in Mexico and could not make
it. What could I do? I could not give their psychological
workshop, and yet I could not offer anything too Eastern—who would understand? Could I translate the Eastern approach to symbolism into a Western approach?
That is how I created my first self-development workshop to help people work with their own personal symbolism.[1]

---

[1] This was the beginning of the LifeSeal workshop, a self-development workshop which is still offered at Yasodhara Ashram. In the
LifeSeal you draw symbols for your own characteristics (including
senses, likes, and dislikes) and arrange them into a whole. Then, with
the help of a group leader, you explore your symbolism, discovering in
this way the guidance from the unconscious.

Then I understood why I had had the dream—because I would really have to listen with the third ear in the workshop. And that is what I did. I got the material from the individual, listened to the individual, asked questions and kept on asking questions, listening for what might not have been spoken aloud.

After such a dream, say thank you. If you can say thank you, you will have more clear dreams. Give your Higher Self recognition. Be very conscientious with your dreams. That will help you to understand. And the more cooperation you give, the more cooperation you will receive. But first you have to give. It is similar to being in a musical conservatory—the more demanding the studies, the fewer the pupils. And if you do not put in the required effort, how can you expect to become a virtuoso? Why should the achievement be dropped into your lap? Even if you are born with a talent, you still have to acquire certain techniques.

If you want clear dreams, simply pray to get the message straight. When we do get the message straight, we are often so shocked by what it tells us that we need to pray for the strength to deal with what has been revealed. We have to be courageous and humble at the same time—courageous enough to face the messages and humble enough to realize that we cannot handle all these problems by ourselves, that we need some Grace. By recognizing humbly that we need Grace, it comes. Then our lives really begin to change.

$\sim$

Our unconscious makes great efforts to get the message through—any dream is an effort. And every dream has meaning. Some dreams may seem to be mainly a review of the day's events, but they are reviewing in order to give you a message. For example, if you have a dream in which you are doing the same activity that you did during the day, you might dismiss the dream, thinking that your mind is just being mechanical—stuck and repeating a thought over and over again. But look for a significance beyond that. Let us say that in your work you have to write letters or design pamphlets, and you find yourself doing this in your dream. Watch to see if one aspect of the dream is trying to teach you how to do the work faster or with better quality, or is showing you an alternative way of accomplishing the task.

Nothing is extraneous or meaningless in dreams. Every part has significance—you just have to go into it more carefully. If you have a dream of receiving invoices and putting the records on the computer, which is the same activity you were doing all day, start by asking yourself, "What does 'invoice' mean to me?" In plain English: writing a bill. My question would be, "If you receive many bills, did you pay them, or did you just put them onto the computer of your mind?" The dream can also be the goad that starts you thinking about the debts you have accumulated. You may not have recognized the *karmic debts* you need to pay.[2] In prayer or meditation you can ask, "What have I misunderstood and what must I do to correct it?" Our human nature is a part of us, but we can subject it to the divine aspect by trying to correct our mistakes.

---

[2] Karma refers to cause and effect, or actions and the results of our actions. If our actions are based on selfishness, greed, pride, self-will, and they cause harm to others, we create a "debt"—something that must be paid back or corrected through appropriate action. In Eastern thinking we have to pay off all karmic debts before we can attain Liberation.

Perhaps as you think about it, you might recognize that through your focus on intellect (the computer), you have created too many debts, which might not have been necessary if you had been directed by your heart. Then you might get a flash about the word "invoice," or *in voice: I have to start to listen to my inner voice.*

Do not assume that a dream is just a repetition of some daily activity or that it comes from a "lower" aspect of mind. The unconscious can be using the language that you understand in order to give you an important message. Be serious and be earnest about your dream work, especially if you say you wish to be in touch with the Guru within or the God within. These are beautiful words, but they are empty if they have no meaning that can be usefully applied in daily living. Really examine yourself to see if you are sincere about wanting to become a spiritual being. It takes time, and you also have to assess yourself correctly.

The message of a dream will not be repeated in the same way if you have rejected it the first time. The unconscious is very creative and will present it differently, until finally you wonder why you had six dreams in a row without understanding the messages. You can be assured those six dreams all had the same message.

I had a student who brought to class a series of dreams that she could not understand. In the first dream, she appeared in court, where the judge ordered her to take off her clothes. She thought, "I cannot stand here naked." In a second dream a police officer ordered her to take off all her clothes, and she would not. Then she had a dream in which she visited a friend who invited her for a swim in her pool, but she had no bathing suit with her and, in fact, was wearing a fur coat. Her friend called to her, "Come and join me in the pool. The water is beautiful. Why don't you take off your fur coat? You can take your clothes off, too. It doesn't matter." She could not.

She had one more dream in which she was staying in a motel and her friends were all going surfing. They were naked and they wanted her to come along, "You will see. It's great!" She did not. Instead she went back to her motel room, which was dark, and went to bed. Then she started to hear all sorts of strange noises and became very frightened, thinking that someone was trying to break in or peek through the window.

In her daily life, this woman worked with other people as a therapist. She asked others to reveal their fears and problems to her, but her own fear of criticism, judgment, and exposure was tremendous. The dreams were showing her how unwilling she was to expose herself (to be naked), and that if she would expose herself, she would gain more understanding of the problems that other people have, and she would also find a greater freedom. When she read the dreams out loud, the whole class understood the message immediately.

It is preferable to work with a series of dreams rather than with just one. It can be risky to work on only one dream and to assess your whole life from the picture it has created. That would be unfair. You are more than what that one dream presents. Even if the dream is pointing out a great mistake, you are more than your mistakes. We all make mistakes occasionally, and many mistakes are bound to happen because we learn by trial and error. So always look at a number of dreams.

But if you have one dream that has recurred throughout your life, you can be sure that it has an extraordinarily important message which you have not understood or acknowledged. Gather all the recurrences of the dream together and study them very carefully. Then before you go to sleep, ask yourself, "What is the message of the dreams?"

Sometimes we can have a dream and understand everything but one small part, as in the following dream of mine.

The House with a Huge Foundation

As I walked along a highway, I saw a cliff of solid rock, and on the rock, a huge foundation for a house that was being built. What is this house standing on? Rock and then huge cedar tree trunks as tall as I am, bound together. I thought, My goodness! This house has an incredible foundation—built on rock with those tremendous cedar logs, which do not rot. I really want to know who lives here. Maybe I will ask the people if I can see their house.

So I climbed up the hill to the door, thinking, "This house is terrific. What a foundation—rock and cedar."

There didn't seem to be anybody here but workmen. One of them turned to me and said, "The house is very solid. Would you like to come in and see it? You will be living here. It's your house."

"My house?"

Oh, I was overjoyed! With that foundation!

I came into a beautiful big room. Then he said, "There are more rooms. Why don't you keep going through? Just watch—there is fresh paint on the doorframe. It's still wet."

But while he was saying this I already had a faint streak of white paint on my coat.

"Oh, we can clean that up," he said, and dipped a cloth into paint remover and wiped it off easily. "But be careful."

I thanked him. Then I went through the house. It was magnificent—big rooms, big windows. I felt a tremendous sense of joy.

I woke up with an elated feeling. This tremendous foundation! Maybe I didn't need to worry so much about my mistakes, and perhaps much of the criticism I received didn't apply. My spiritual house has a good foundation! The dream was a tremendous boost in a very difficult time. When you live and work with people and really want to help them, sometimes it is the biggest job you can think of.

But the white paint—I couldn't understand what the white paint symbolized. At least, I thought, it is white, a good color—purity, transparency. It can't be all that bad; I'll leave it for now.

Six months later I had another dream:

The Affirming Song

A voice was singing the words of a popular song, "I believe in the goodness of all." Then someone handed me a piece of paper with a date on it.

I woke up and remembered the numbers. So I looked up my dream from that date, and it was

*the dream about the house with the great founda-
tion and the paint on my coat.*

Suddenly I began to understand, and this is why it
is so important to keep a diary or to write down something about our daily activity and what is going on in
the mind. At the time of the first dream, we had just
moved the ashram to the country, the weather was beautiful, and I was overjoyed to be able to walk around our
own land, with so many new and beautiful things to
discover. I did not like to be sitting inside at the typewriter answering the same types of letters from people
who were just expressing their dislike, their negativity,
their resentment. I was dealing with the same problems
over and over—people's own selfishness: "My husband
..." "My wife ... " "My daughter ... " "My son ..." "My
boss ... " Everybody was to blame except themselves.
So I was feeling somewhat resentful that I had to answer one more letter from one particular woman who
just would not give up. I sat at the typewriter and I could
not think of a single thing to say. Then I realized, "Yes, I
know why I can't write. I am being too critical." So to
correct my attitude I typed out a whole page of "I shall
not criticize."

This was the white paint. This was the mistake.
Knowing about the polarity of the mind, I should have
realized that I was reinforcing my sense of criticism by
writing in this negative form. It was really negligence.
Instead of replacing the idea of criticism with greater
depth of understanding, more patience, I had made a
negative suggestion to myself. The second dream gave

me the positive alternative: "I believe in the goodness of all."

But it was six months before I got this help. Sometimes we think if we have not understood the message we will receive help within a week. I have discovered that this is not always the case.

So we have to watch our dreams very carefully, with great attention. Occasionally when I have recorded a dream I have put down the wrong year. Instead of dismissing it I have looked up the year. What was happening for me then? What could the message be?

The dream does not say, "Two and two is four and one is five." We have to increase our intuition and our interest in ourselves to a much greater degree if we want to pick up the messages from the unconscious.

6

Reviewing & Classifying Dreams

IKE SCIENTISTS WHO check their calculations, we also have to check out our dream
interpretations. Make time once a week for
reading over your dreams of the week.
This is a way of putting self-importance, which is often
misplaced in socializing, into the right place. When you
become important enough to yourself to know yourself, you will become important to others because you
will truly have something to give.

Take your whole book of dreams each year and set
aside a week to read it over, adding your new interpretations and insights on separate pages. With the distance
in time and the increase of your understanding, you will

be able to be more specific and see with greater clarity. You will also have the benefit of discovering your own process of growth. If someone else tells you that you have developed, you will think they are just trying to humor you, but here the evidence is in your own writing. Little by little, you will see the changes that you have undergone. It is as if you were a little child, and as you grow you need bigger shoes and larger clothes; only here the growing needs bigger dreams. By keeping up your dream diary and adding insights from time to time, you receive confirmation that you really have made the grade. If you look at life as a big schoolhouse, you will see you have passed this grade and can move on to another level.

You may find your dreams have changed in meaning. When you stay involved with self-discovery, you re-evaluate everything that has taken place in your life. You may discover that you have grown in conviction and in faith, including faith in yourself, and that you are still moving toward your goal. Eventually you will see that you have become a new person. But you cannot reach this point without ruthless honesty. You have to meet yourself on the gut level.

You also have to have the humility to see that your development grows slowly—by inches, not by miles. You need to review the dreams continually to remind yourself of what you have already learned. If you go back to your first recorded dreams five or even ten years later, you will see how much you have forgotten. Reviewing keeps you in touch with what you already know and gives you another chance to put it into action.

You may discover a higher level in some dreams, and see in retrospect your limited understanding and misinterpretations and sometimes intentional blindness, when you did not really want to see what a dream was telling you. Then you can ask yourself, "What is a dream?"—particularly if you want to take that step of seeing that daily living is just another form of dream.

~

As you review your dreams, list the different types of dreams you have. Then you can begin to classify them into categories. The categories you choose have to be your own because you want to understand the workings of your own mind. By grouping together similar dreams and dream symbols, you will gradually learn to recognize the type of dream you have had soon after you have dreamed it. When you can discern which are anxiety dreams, which are prophetic, which are wishful thinking, which are instructive dreams, then you can really start using your dreams to help you make decisions. Through systematically studying the process of your unconscious in this way, you will also increase intuitive perception and gain greater awareness.

To begin to compile your classification system, you can either make copies of your dreams or work with them on a computer. If you enter all your dreams onto a computer, you can easily select the key words and the dates you had the dreams while maintaining the original order. You might choose to look at all the people that you know, people that you do not know, animals, buildings (houses, hotels, restaurants, office buildings), vehicles. Then you can study each category. If the category is animals, how many different animals appeared in your dreams? Which animal did you dream of most often? What is the symbolic meaning of that animal to you? What are the characteristics of the animal?

In the overview of a particular symbol, you can again trace your personal development. Perhaps as you look at the buildings in your dreams, you will see that at one time many of the houses were quite flimsy; then they became more solid. Or perhaps there was once a room that no longer exists; this could indicate that something is finished and you no longer need to worry about it. Or perhaps a small, crowded house has expanded with new additions. You can see your life story in a condensed way and make a new assessment of your present situation.

You may want to look at dreams with similar symbols and try to condense the message of several dreams into one, because the same message may have been given many times, but you did not understand it.

In your classification of dreams you may choose to work with just a few major categories—for example health dreams, psychological dreams, and instructive dreams. Or you can create as many categories as you become aware of. There could be categories such as: Food, Sickness, Healing, Sex, Spiritual Guidance and Inspiration, Memories and Past Lives, Death and Birth, Problem-Solving (business problems, family problems, emotional problems), Shared Dreams (with a loved one or a friend), Prophetic Dreams, and Instructive Dreams.

You can group together dreams in color, dreams with intensely vivid colors, dreams in black and white.

Examine your senses in your dreams. Which senses were active? Do people speak in your dreams? Do you see and hear them at the same time? What about smell, taste, and touch? Do you experience these senses in your dreams? Which senses are missing? Group together the dreams in which the same sense is active. Through this kind of examination, you can discover which of your senses is dominant and which need developing. You might see which senses work together and which compete.

Moses Maimonides, a twelfth century Jewish philosopher, classified prophecies into twelve degrees, and gave examples of at least one dream or vision in each category from the Old Testament.[1] At some point, you may find it rewarding to divide your own dreams into sub-categories in a similar way. If you do this, you will gain a tremendous knowledge of your unconscious. Your list might include: Clairvoyant Dreams, Precognitive Dreams, Telepathic Dreams, Warnings in Dreams, Premonitions about your own Death.

As you work with your classification system, however, always keep one set of dreams in chronological

---

[1] Moses Maimonides. *Guide of the Perplexed, Book I,* Friedlander, trans. (New York: Dover, 1956), 240-245.

In summary, Maimonides said the twelve degrees of prophecy were:

1. When the spirit of the Lord comes and one is inspired by God to do some grand or good action.

2. Speaking and writing by the holy spirit, when one starts to speak words of wisdom and praise, while fully conscious and in the wakened state.

3. When the picture in a dream is explained in the dream itself, as for example in the dream of Zechariah

4. When one hears speech in a dream but does not see the speaker, for example, Samuel at the beginning of his prophetic mission.

5. When one is spoken to by another person in the dream, as in some of the prophecies of Ezekiel.

6. When an angel speaks to one in a dream, which is said to be the condition of most prophets.

order. There is a significance to the order in which you have your dreams in the same way that there is a significance in the way your life progresses. You would not celebrate your sixty-fifth birthday when you are only forty. You live your life in a certain sequence, and by following your dreams through this sequence you can see the flow in which you become open and receptive. It can be very beautiful to observe how your Higher Self puts in the effort, and what happens when you cooperate with your Higher Self.

Mind the interpreter goes on and on, which is why we have so many dreams. Most of the time we do not get the message straight. As you find out that dreams are giving it to you straight, you will discover that your unconscious has a very definite language. As you learn the language, you will have fewer problems with interpretation. And if you have a deep dedication to spiritual life, your Higher Self will prevent you from making foolish mistakes that would slow your progress.

The following chapters—Dreams of Enjoyment, Suffering, Birth and Death, Nightmares, Decision-Making Dreams, Prophetic Dreams, Warning Dreams, Dream Sharing, Past Lives and Dreams, and Dreams of Spiritual Guidance—are just a few of the possibilities for categorizing dreams that I explore in more detail. I

---

7. When it seems that God is speaking to one in a dream, as in Isaiah.

8. When a vision appears to one, and he sees a picture, as in Genesis.

9. When one hears words in a vision, as in Genesis.

10. When one sees a man speaking to him in a vision, as happened to Joshua in Jericho.

11. When one sees an angel speaking to him in a vision, as was the case when Abraham was addressed by an angel at the sacrifice of Isaac.

12. When one sees God speaking to him in a vision, as happened to Moses.

have included examples from my own dreams and from people with whom I have worked in order to illustrate the principles discussed and to open up your own thinking and investigation. Please remember that to expand your awareness and self-knowledge, you should classify your dreams into categories based on what you understand from your own dreams.

7

Dreams of Enjoyment, Suffering, Birth & Death

WE CAN GAIN an awareness of both our emotional life and our spiritual life by studying the range of our emotional responses in dreams, from despair to delight; and by seeing the range of opposites, from birth to death.

As long as we are in a human body we will have emotions, but we cannot let our negative emotions carry us away. There are many tragic examples where an emotion like revenge can carry on for generations in family feuds or religious conflicts. We can attain balance in life through what I call "the foundation work" or self-examination, which clears away many of the obstacles on the way to the Higher Self. We need to see when emotions overpower us and acknowledge that we have to do something about them.

As you continue to develop, you will continue to have new insights and expanded awareness. The sensitive emotions that originally created feelings of pain will undergo a transformation, and you will be able to identify the finer feelings of the heart. Whereas the emotions can experience a pain that rips you apart, the heart will experience only a feeling of sadness in the same event. From the types of dreams we have, we will see what we should do and how we should look at things.

Dreams can also be a reliving of an unpleasant or pleasurable event, or a release of the emotions that we have not dealt with. Because we are endowed with consciousness, we should look into our dreams and find out why we are laughing or crying.

We can have dreams in which we suffer. In that case, ask yourself, "What is the pain? Is it imagined pain? Was I really only inconvenienced?" You can feel hurt and let down when the other person had no intention of hurting you—you were hurt only because you counted on something that is now not going to happen. If you feel hurt, you may cry. What kind of tears? Self-pity, healing, grief, bitterness? Find out what is behind your tears.

You may literally cry in your sleep and wake up in tears. If you have a dream in which you really sob and do not know why—all you remember is an intense feeling of sadness—it is important to see what is being brought to your awareness. Something in you is suffering. Look at your suffering and ask, "Do I still need to

shed tears, but my pride won't allow me to cry?" Could it be your soul crying because it is not heard? I feel that the poorest Hindu servants I met were often better off than the very learned pundits because it is very difficult to overcome pride unless you allow yourself to be devotional. That is what the dream may be showing you: if you have no reason to cry—nobody died, you have no pain, you have no other fears or premonitions—it could be your own soul, the Higher Self, that is crying out. You have to clarify this for yourself.

Your dreams will also reflect your positive feelings of enjoyment. You had a marvelous time. You felt wonderful! You wake up in a happy mood. In the dream you may have been riding the crest of the wave.

Occasionally when circumstances in my life were very difficult, I would have a dream of Krishna as a baby or young child. These dreams, such as the following one, would give me a tremendous feeling of joy and delight.

Baby Krishna

I am in a room that is quite dimly lit. In the far corner it is extremely dark, but I can just make out something moving on the floor.

Oh! It's a baby! No cushion! No blanket! And I think, Now who would put a baby on a bare floor without protection?

Then this little one crawls over to me, pulls himself up on my sari, and looks at me with big loving eyes.

"Oh! You are Krishna!"

The moment I recognize him, he disappears.

Of course it was delightful to see God in the form of this baby, so trusting, crawl directly to me. This was a dream of great enjoyment, a dream that awakened wonder and returned a sense of balance to my life.

⌒

We can also look at birth and death in dreams. Many times a baby is born, which often means that the inner being wants to manifest. And it makes itself known as a tiny baby because such a small creature is non-threatening. If the dream conveyed a huge or dramatic experience, some people would panic. If you dreamed about the Buddha and eventually interpreted the image to mean the state beyond mind, you might think, "I don't know anything beyond the mind. It could be terrible. I might lose my individuality. What will become of *me?* I know myself only through my mind."

When we dream about babies, we may be told that we have to protect them. You know how tender and vulnerable the baby is, and how it depends on your care. This is true for a newly-emerging spiritual life, too.

I have met several men who dreamed of giving birth. They were quite surprised. One gave birth in front of a fireplace. Why, I wondered, in front of the fireplace? Did he want the baby to enjoy the warmth of the fire, or did some part of him want to throw the baby into the fire and get rid of it? He had to find out for himself, but the implications were clear: either he would accept what had recently come to life in himself with loving warmth, or he would reject and destroy it. If his feelings were negative, at least he could honestly recognize his hostility toward spiritual life and acknowledge that it was finished. On the other hand if he responded enthusiastically—"It's great! I'm not a woman, yet I can give birth, and the fire will keep this little one warm"—this would indicate his willingness to accept the birth of a new awareness.

If we have enjoyment, suffering, and birth in dreams, what about death? If you see dead bodies or a sarcophagus or casket, do not make the mistake of thinking that you will die tomorrow. I have died many times in my dreams and I am still here! Something else has to die, and something has to be willing to let it die. If you have a personality aspect that is jealous and acts very badly, would you not rather let that personality aspect die? But that does not mean *you* die. And do not wake up old ghosts. The past is the past.

What if you dream you have killed somebody? "You may become upset and say to yourself, I have done all this practice but here in my dream I have killed somebody!" This could be a positive dream. If the individual you killed was a personality aspect that created a lot of obstacles in your life, it needed to be killed. But if you really identify with that personality aspect, you may worry and wonder, "Does the dream announce that *I* am going to die?" That worry shows your attachment to the personality aspect.

When you kill someone in your dream, what is the motivation? If you kill your grandfather or your uncle, what do these people symbolize? Are they a substitute for someone else? Do you really want to kill your husband or lover or boss? Such dreams can arise when you use language carelessly, if you often say, for example, "I could *kill* this guy."

You have to look at the person you are killing. Do you consider him arrogant? In that case killing him would really mean destroying your own arrogance, which needs to be destroyed. However, if you have strong feelings of revenge, you have to ask yourself, "What right do I have to attack others? Maybe I have to deal with my own arrogance before I confront somebody else."

A very devout Christian once told me about going into a Catholic Church, seeing a life-sized image of Jesus, and suddenly realizing, "I, too, even today, contribute again and again to the crucifixion by not living up to my highest ideals." Are you killing the holiness in yourself?

How can you know when a dream of death is symbolic and when it is prophetic? If, through working on yourself, you have changed your relationship with your mother, for example, you may have a dream that your mother is dying. The old image of your mother in your mind has died. If the dream was a premonition rather than being symbolic, you would probably act differently. You would feel anxious, and you may write or phone her to reassure yourself. The feeling tone of the dream is often a good indicator. But sometimes it is very obvious: when you have changed an old attitude, an old image can die.

Sometimes when a dream is prophetic there may not be a particularly distinct feeling tone. A few years ago I had a dream in which I was showing people some photographs. There were several women in one picture, and one woman stood out more than the others; but none of their faces meant anything to me. Someone asked, "Oh, is this a picture of your mother?"

I said, "No, she's not in the picture."

And I knew when I woke up that my mother had died. There was no strong feeling in the dream—"It's over!"—but simply, "She's not in the picture." She was very unhappy when I was born because she had never wanted children, and she had not been in contact with me since I took my initiation into *sanyas*.[1] I continued to keep her in my prayers and in the Light, and I had the sense that she would gradually move toward the Light.

Dreams provide us with a reflection of our current emotional, mental, and spiritual states. With this information we can take action in our daily lives to overcome what must be overcome, and to move toward the promises given.

---

[1] *Sanyas* refers to renunciation of action based on desire. A sanyasin is called a swami and given a new name.

8

Nightmares

NIGHTMARES USUALLY indicate unre-
solved problems. I have observed that
people who have many nightmares are
usually the most resistant to doing anything to improve their lives. They are stubborn beyond
any logic. In other words, the little boy or little girl in
them says, "No—I don't have to change!" Some nightmares reflect just that state of mind. However, if the person begins meditating, chanting, or praying, he or she
may start to understand more about humility and gratitude, and the nightmares will disappear.

If you have threatening dreams consecutively over
several nights, there is definitely something wrong in

your thinking. Maybe there is too much resentment, or too much resistance to good influences, or a refusal to listen—even to earlier dreams. The threatening dream gives the message: "You either listen, *or else*. Accept the challenge and work with it and meet the challenge, *or else*."

If you always blame other people and refuse to take responsibility for your own actions and emotions, you may have dreams in which you are chased by monsters or some other force. In waking life it is always, "Somebody else made a mistake." "If she hadn't forgotten . . . ." "If he were more intelligent or accommodating . . . ." *You* never make mistakes. *Your* selfishness and greed never need to be trimmed. It is always everybody else's fault. In the office, people blame each other constantly. Husband and wife blame each other. Many people blame their parents: "They have done this to me."

When you blame other people and refuse to accept a responsibility that is entirely your own, you will have one disaster in life after another. You contribute to your own disasters. Your life becomes the nightmare. If you make a decision that for the next three months you will not blame anybody else for anything, and instead you will ask where *you* have not been accurate, when *you* have not been on time, or where *your* instructions were sloppy—you will find that the contents of your dreams will also change.

One person I knew who could not accept responsibility for her actions and, because of false pride, always blamed others, told me that she had a recurring dream in which a little girl was wandering alone in a vast desert, not knowing where to go. Everything looked barren.

This woman's tendency to blame others had indeed made life around her very barren and empty, and had reduced her to a small child who could not find her way home, because there was no home. Images of being attacked in a dream, as well as symbolizing your tendency to attack, can also arise from the unconcious influence of those people on whom you lay all the blame.

If you often dream of being chased, find out who is chasing you. Being chased by the police could indicate either that you are very critical and judgmental of other people or that you are doing some wrong action that you have to deal with in waking life. You may be chased by one of your personality aspects or one of your own characteristics that you criticize in another person, even someone from the past. That personality aspect should definitely be dealt with. Either it needs to be conquered or it needs to be nourished. If it is one which needs to be nourished and you meet that need, this aspect may eventually become a kind of guide on the spiritual path.

Some nightmares may be warnings about selfishness, symbolized as a monster running after you who wants to sink its big fangs into your neck and squeeze the life out of you. The dramatic impact of the dream brings the message: "It's *time!* Hurry up. Expand your life. Give something back to life!"

One student of mine had many dreams about men attacking her or abusing her in some way. But after working with her dreams and facing herself courageously for a number of years, she had the following dream.

The Man Crouched in the Sewer Pipe
I was walking past a large sewer pipe that was lying on the ground. It was quite dark, and I could see somebody

crouched in there. Was he ready to attack? My instinct was to run away. Then I thought, "No, I want to see what it is." I bent down and looked in, and there was a very ugly, revolting man. But as I looked at him more intently, he reached up and peeled a mask off his face. Underneath was a very friendly, pleasant looking man.

The dreamer interpreted her dream as follows: "Of course I had a feeling of acceptance and great relief. The dream was telling me very clearly that if I could look at the ugly parts of myself and really acknowledge them, I would find underneath a friendly, helpful person. So over the years these threatening characters in my dreams gradually became friendly aspects on whom I could call for help."

If you have dreams that are threatening and you are aware that you are dreaming, by all means wake yourself up. You can affirm to yourself, "I know it is only a dream." Try to look beyond the negativity and direct your mind to the positive. Instead of battling the darkness, begin to invite the Light into your mind. Always look up to the Light because darkness will not follow you into Light. On the other hand, if you try to fight evil, it will draw you down. So when you wake up, realize that you have a choice—to step into darkness or to step into the Light.

Some people do not know they are dreaming, and others can wake themselves up from a nightmare; still others, who have awareness that they are dreaming, can change the course of action in the dream itself. Different temperaments do different things.

One woman had the following dream.

Big Waves

I went to a summer resort and was ready to go in for a swim. The water seemed quite calm, but suddenly huge waves came up. I cowered, curling up, frightened that I would get dragged out to sea. The small lake had become a tumultuous ocean.

As she worked with the dream, the woman admitted that she tended to feel crushed by the "big waves" of life—the sudden changes, the emotional dramas. I helped her to explore options. What other way could she respond to changes in her life? How did her own emotions create tumultuous conditions? By consciously exploring options, she created a choice for herself. She no longer needed to become paralyzed by her fear.

If a child frequently wakes up with nightmares, it indicates a great insecurity. Parents should find out what the child fears. Listening to your children's dreams can give you good insights into how to help them.

Similarly, if you have frequent nightmares, explore your own fears. Working consciously to overcome your fears will free you from the psychological tension that creates the nightmares. When you clear the space, you allow room for a different kind of dream, a more subtle message from the unconscious. Nightmares are like an alarm. Pay attention to the alarm. Take action in your life.

9

Decision-Making Dreams

YOU MUST BE willing to make an important decision consciously, not relying solely on your dreams. Many times dreams do not suggest what your decision should be because you are first meant to think about your choices and make the decision on a conscious level. Once you have made your decision, you can use your dreams as a comparison. Even then, do not act on only one single dream; see if the same message comes in other dreams. In this way you will be assured that you are not responding from wishful thinking and the creativity of your own mind.

When you think through your choices consciously, first assess your emotional satisfaction. If your emotional gratification is high enough you will be willing to make certain sacrifices. But realistically anticipate the problems that could arise. Take into account the shortcomings and handicaps that your decision will bring. Then say yes or no, and let your dreams be the confirmation or opposition.

If, for example, you are trying to decide about whether to accept a teaching position at the university as your sole activity, or whether to quit teaching and work only as an artist, wait for the dreams to confirm or oppose the decision. You can affirm to yourself, "My unconscious knows already, so please show me. I will read the signs through what you say." Then accept the dream as it comes.

But for your own peace of mind, you can even oppose the decision that comes through your dreams. Review once again what the repercussions of the decision would be and how you would feel about them, so that if you decide to be an artist without a regular income, you will not say later, "Maybe I made a mistake. Maybe I misunderstood the message from the dream."

Dreams can help you make the decision, but the unconscious will only give you the message if you are receptive. If you have no openness to what your dreams offer, in effect you are telling your Higher Self that you will not accept anything contrary to your decision. So you will not get the message from the unconscious. The dreams will only come if the Higher Self knows that you will accept them. If you fight, if you deny, if you justify, of course the help will not come in a dream; you will not listen to the opposite viewpoint.

Suppose you ask, "Should I stay at Yasodhara Ashram even for a short time?" Then you think, "No, this would create too much trouble. I wouldn't see my boyfriend," or, "My husband might get angry," or, "What would my boss say?" or, "How would my wife look at this?" And something in you keeps saying, "Maybe I should stay. Maybe it will help me to break loose from old habits." You will receive help in a dream only if your desire to stay is greater than your anxiety about your family or career. Otherwise, the Higher Self will not respond because you do not want to hear the message. You are just toying with the idea.

You could also make the opposite decision. You may think, "I don't want to go back home to that dreadful atmosphere. I think I'll stay here at the ashram where it's beautiful, and the people are nice, and I don't have to cook or wash dishes. I wish somebody would tell me if it is the right thing to do. Wouldn't it be great if the answer came in a dream?" The answer will not come. And the fact that you do not receive the dream you want is also the answer. When you have too great a fear or too much ambition or you have already made the decision based on self-will or a desire to escape, the Higher Self knows that you will not listen. So why say it? You may get the message at some other time—perhaps a year later when you have drifted away from the intensity of the fear or the ambition.

If the dream itself conveys a fear, a decision should not be made as long as you are fearful. Wait and investigate further, and perhaps you will find what needs to be discovered. In the example I gave earlier of the engineer's dream,[1] the dream showed him that what he planned to do was arising from a state of confusion and would lead to nonsensical results. The dream could lead him to postponing the decision, at least until his confusion was clarified.

If your dreams are so confused or so elaborate and detailed that you cannot understand the message, this could indicate that you really do not want to hear the answer. Wishful thinking can also produce a dream, so you have to learn to discriminate between different types of dreams.

I always advise people to ask, "What is in the divine plan? Open the doors if you want me to do this." Even that may not tell you with absolute certainty because you can believe that the door is open when it really is not. You can misinterpret the message if you want to do something very badly. Be very vigilant in your daily reflections. Do not let self-will interfere. If you want a clear-cut answer from your own divine being, you must clarify for yourself whether or not you are willing to follow the instructions you receive. You can tell the Divine, "I will go wherever you want me to go and do the work you want me to do." But you can only say that if you really agree to do what is asked, whatever the work is.

If, in making a decision, you rely on two, three, or four dreams, and also on what emerges in your own thinking and reflections, you will gain a greater sense of assurance. Only if you are very clear that you are acting

---

[1] See page 21

from a level of spontaneous inner response should you take action based on one single dream. But you have to know the difference between acting compulsively from an emotional level and acting spontaneously from an intuitive insight. People often confuse the two and are afraid they will lose their spontaneity, but this is not the case. Dreams can show you whether you have acted spontaneously or whether you have been forced by your emotions to act and have thereby given your emotions too much power.

Dreams have helped me make decisions in areas in which I had no background, such as in building construction and finances. I would not even have recognized the choices available without their help. Dreams have also shown me when I should enter a different phase of my work—for example, when I should start writing.

The following dream, "The Queens Dream," is a personal example of how the Divine not only works with us, but also works for us, sometimes in spite of ourselves.

THE QUEENS DREAM

For six and a half years I had faithfully written down my dreams and worked intensively with them, but one night I decided that I wanted to sleep right through. Ashram activities were quite demanding and I was very tired. Besides, I thought, my dreams have given me more than enough material for the rest of my life.

So that night when I became aware that I was dreaming I said, "No, no. I'm not going to write it down. I want to sleep through. I feel tired . . . very, very tired."

My dream voice answered, "Okay, but just write these two things down: *the Queen of the Bees* and *the Queen of England.*" So in my sleepy state I found my pencil and scribbled down the words.

I could barely read them the next morning since I had written in the dark, and had not been in a particularly cooperative frame of mind. I finally deciphered my writing—*the Queen of the Bees* and *the Queen of England.*

I thought, "What can I possibly do with these two fragments? Ridiculous. The Queen of England? I lived for a year in England and I saw the coronation of Elizabeth. I thought I had never seen a sadder queen. She seemed to be weighed down by the mantle put on her shoulders. What does this mean? Do I feel weighed down? Yes, sometimes, but I am not so unaware of it that I would have to dream about it. What does this have to do with the Queen of the Bees? I have no idea about bees. I have nothing to do with them." So I tossed the dream into a drawer where I kept the others and did not think of it further.

Several months passed. One night I went down to the ashram dining room and found that dinner was late. Something must have happened, and I was very eager to get into the kitchen to help. There were many visitors, and I did not want to keep them waiting, but as I walked into the dining room one of my guests fanatically insisted on engaging me in a conversation which I certainly was not interested in. He was a tall fellow and had reached to the top of the bookshelves and found a little pocketbook. He said, "Oh, Swami Radha, what a lovely book! I would like to read this to you." I was thinking, "It is much more important to get into the kitchen and lend a hand." But there I was—caught.

"It's called *The Life of the Bee,* by Maeterlinck.[2] Listen to this. Most fascinating." Standing up in the middle of the room, he read the whole chapter on the life of the Queen of the Bees. I was startled. The Queen of the Bees—my dream . . . . I did not even know this book existed. It was one of the books that belonged to the previous owners of the property who had not bothered to pick them up. Still, I thought, I can't see how this Queen of the Bees applies to me. Besides, I was very distracted with the idea of getting dinner ready, and I hardly listened. A few ideas stayed with me, but I never got around to picking up the book again and reading it for myself.

Now see what tremendous efforts the Higher Self will make to get an important message across to us? About one year later, I was in Oregon at the invitation of an artist who lived in the country outside Portland. I was there only this one time. She had asked me to stay with her on my way to San Francisco and had invited some friends to join us for dinner in her very lovely house.

There was a little envelope on my dinner plate and she asked me to open it before she served the food. I thought it was probably a question about something she wanted to discuss personally or perhaps a thank you note for coming. I opened the letter and what did I see?

"Dear Swami Radha: I have just read Maeterlinck's *Life of the Bee,* and this passage struck me so much that

---

[2] Maurice Maeterlinck. *The Life of the Bee.* Alfred Sutro, trans. (New York: The New American Library, 1954).

I felt compelled to write it down for you. I'm sure you will know why."

Yes, did I ever!

What did it say? The life of the Queen of the Bees is a very peculiar one. She cannot be compared to our worldly queens. She does the work because it needs to be done, even though there is no honor or reward in it. The queen is sealed up with all the eggs of the young bees, and she nourishes them with her own substance. She rears new princesses, and at the proper time they leave the hive.[3]

What is my substance? Only the spiritual message. I have no other resources with which to nourish any-one. There really must be something in that dream.

At the end of the same summer, a very nice lady from England stopped by the ashram. She said, "I bring you greetings from your friends in England. They spoke so highly of you that I wanted to come and bring you something special. But I didn't know what you would like—you seem to live quite a different life from the rest of us." She went on, "The only thing I could think of was this—the first Jubilee magazine of the Queen of England."

I really cannot describe how this gripped me. I had never seen this woman before and I never saw her again. I do not even remember her name. She was here for one afternoon on her way to Vancouver and had come to deliver a magazine about the Queen of England . . . because I was not paying attention to this dream frag-ment: *the Queen of the Bees* and *the Queen of England.* What a tremendous effort the Divine was making to get

[3] Maeterlinck, *Life of the Bee*, 25-26

a message across—even delivering this poor woman into our remote region in the mountains!

When I opened the magazine, the first thing I read was that the Queen of England is the only woman who cannot speak back. The next paragraph said that she is the head of state and the first woman of the country, but the work is carried out by the Parliament's Upper and Lower Houses. The queen knows all the secrets of state, but only in the most important instances will she make a final decision or cast the deciding vote.

~

The Queens dream turned out to be very important to me and settled some questions I had been pondering over for years. I was doing some long-term thinking about the structure of the ashram and trying to decide how to distribute the work. Up to this time I had been in charge of the administration of the ashram, but I felt it was necessary to bring the residents into more responsible positions. I wanted to distribute authority among them so they could play an active role in the place where they lived. Also, if individuals decided to leave the ashram, they would have gained confidence and assurance in handling their lives and would not feel stranded and helpless because everything had always been laid out for them.

I had mixed thoughts and feelings. I wanted people to learn to take responsibility, but my sense of duty also made me question whether I was just trying to escape work that was not particularly inspiring. When I had first tentatively approached a few people and asked, "What are you interested in? What would you like to take on? Would you like to teach?" one person responded, "Are you just looking for the easy way out?"

I had to ask myself, "Am I?" Did I want to escape work that was really mine? Did I just want to hand over the parts I did not like? Or had I deteriorated to the point where I was sick and tired of doing my duty? Did I consider myself too important to do this work now? What was it? All these thoughts were going around and around in my mind, and I was not quite sure what I should do.

The dream gave me a beautiful answer. This is the way it is: there are structures everywhere in nature and in human society, with the right place for each individual. The dream was saying that capable people will come who will carry out the work. From the Queen of the Bees I learned that I should train more than one, just as the queen bee has more than one princess who will later start another hive. How would I go about bringing other people in? I should follow the political model of the Queen of England. Let the issues be discussed as they are in the Upper and Lower House and then be voted on, and let the decisions stand. That is how the ashram functions today. So the dream assured me that by passing on responsibility, I was not trying to escape.

My Guru had always wanted to see America dotted with many little yoga centers that I would visit, but it seemed more than enough for me to run one ashram. Eventually, however, twenty-five years after my return from India, the centers started to come into being. My dream about the Queen of the Bees training the princesses for the new hives was fulfilled in this sense as well.

But can you see the enormous effort that was involved in getting the message through to me? Who does it? Who takes the time to observe that closely? Who pulls the strings and makes it all happen? Why would that man read a book from the highest shelf? Why was the book there in the first place? Why would the woman in Oregon type out the same passage and give it to me? Why would the woman from England, who never visited again, deliver the information about the Queen? What a job I had created for my Higher Self to complete the message that I had refused to look at, saying, "I'm tired. I want to sleep . . . two queens: *Queen of the Bees, Queen of England.* Ridiculous." See how ridiculous it was? It was the answer to the cardinal question that had worried me for years.

Here was a dream that was not willingly received. But because for years I had put in all my good will and sincerity, when an important message came, my Higher Self insisted that it be heard. My Guru was thousands of miles away, and I could not make my students my confidantes. I came to rely completely on this inner Guru that was awakened through following up on my dreams. But I also did not play with my dreams, trying to manipulate them or pre-determine their messages. I wanted the message only from the Most High. As Jesus said, "If you ask for bread, you will not be given stones."[3] Your Higher Self will not let you down, even if you are not always accepting. I hope you will think about this and trace in your own life the ways in which the Divine has

---

[4] "Or what man is there of you, whom if his son ask bread, will he give him a stone?" Matt. 7:9

arranged extraordinary circumstances for your personal and spiritual development.

After I had accepted the idea that I was not running away from my duties, I had a final dream around this decision.

Names on the Board

I was walking along the familiar territory near the ashram, but instead of the ferry landing, there was an exceptionally big tree. On the tree was a big poster that said, "Vote." And there were a number of names of ashram people listed. I read the names. My name wasn't on the board, but at the bottom of the poster was a note that these people had been chosen by the queen as most suitable for the job.

When I woke up I remembered three of these names and began to intensify the training of these people.

What I want to emphasize with this particular dream is that you have a duty to pay attention and surrender to the direction that comes from the Higher Self. Make up your mind that you want only the Most High. Refuse to accept anything else.

Only the Most High.

10

Prophetic Dreams

C AN WE PREDICT the future? This question has been fiercely debated in every century and in many cultures. Certain things are predictable, such as planting seeds that will grow into a particular fruit at a particular time. The movements of the earth, the moon, and the galaxies have certain rhythms that allow us to predict that day will follow night, that seasons will progress in a certain order, and so on. Modern technology provides doctors with the possibility of predicting, through prenatal testing, whether an unborn child will be healthy or malformed.

But do the possibilities that have already been established allow us to assume that other human events can be predicted? Can we predict whether we will win a lottery, inherit unexpected wealth, have a happy marriage, or win a competition for a high position? Can we predict advances in the medical field or accidents before they happen? Does the human mind know ahead of time the outline of the play?

Many predictions, of course, are not really predictions, but are manipulations by those clever enough to know how we behave when adequately conditioned, as, for example in war, espionage, and politics. Political opponents vie for the last word in a debate because the last word is what will stay in the listeners' or viewers' minds.

How much does the power of suggestion contribute to the fulfillment of a prediction? Some people seem to be so sensitive that any suggestion becomes almost a hypnotic command. But are there other individuals who are so intent on knowing what will unfold that they can indeed perceive future events? To what extent are emotions a contributing factor? Again, this is an area that needs much more exploration.

We can best answer the question of whether prediction is possible by becoming our own laboratory, observing our many feelings and intuitions and those unexpected, illogical thoughts that suddenly surface. Many powers of the mind are still so unexplored that some people will deny the possibility of prophecy, while others will swear by stories they have heard. From my observation, it is only through our own personal interest, pursuit, and follow-through that we will find satisfactory answers.

Dreams definitely open the door to this area and help us safely decipher the psyche and its powers. Dreams give us fuller access to intuitive perception, which in waking consciousness we contact only occasionally and incompletely. As we work with dreams, we may discover that some of them are indeed prophetic, or what we sometimes call "psychic" dreams. The original Greek meaning of *psyche* is soul. So we can look at psychic dreams as a way to have more contact with the soul forces. In order to recognize these dreams, we have to develop our observation of how the unconscious functions and make a special study of the workings of intuitive perception.

Collect your dreams and observe in your diary when a dream turns out to be prophetic. If you do not keep a record, the mind will twist things around over time. What is your feeling when you wake up? What is your frame of mind? Is your intuition asleep or active? Eventually you will know when your dream is prophetic and when the meaning is entirely symbolic.

Many people have dreams that foretell a small event the next day—nothing dramatic—perhaps just seeing an object or encountering a particular person. Again, you have to write the events down and observe when they have accumulated. The small events may finally develop into something more serious. The small events also prepare you, if you are very frightened, to accept this precognitive aspect of mind. For example, if you dream of someone in the morning and that person comes to visit you later in the day, that is non-threatening. After you have a number of non-threatening experiences, you become a little more open to possibilities. The Divine is a gentle teacher.

Abraham Lincoln had a precognitive dream of his own death.[1] Lincoln dreamed that he heard the mournful sound of many people grieving, and when, in his dream, he went into the East Room of the White House he saw a display coffin with candles all around and hundreds of mourners everywhere. When he asked who was dead, the response was, "The President." Several days later Lincoln was assassinated.

People who are assassinated often have some sort of premonition in their dreams. Why is that? What is premonition? We have to understand the interplay of forces. If you scheme something bad against me, I may feel fear arise and look around for the source of my fear, and then have the dream. I may not experience the assassination in the dream, but I may see the result—the dead body—as Lincoln did.

There were several people in the small town near the ashram who had dreams that cars were plunging into the river because the old wooden bridge was collapsing. A few people even wrote to the newspaper to make inquiries about the condition of the bridge and how often it was checked. The response was that the bridge had been checked three months earlier. Unfortunately, however, something had been overlooked.

The wife of a man who drove across the bridge to work every morning said to him, "I feel very uneasy. I don't want you to go to work today." But because she

---

[1] See excerpt from *Recollections of Abraham Lincoln, 1847-1865*, quoted in Stephen Brook, *The Oxford Book of Dreams* (Oxford: Oxford University Press, 1983), 143-144.

could not say why, he dismissed her feelings and left at the usual time. When he came to the bridge, the car in front of him suddenly disappeared. He slammed on his brakes, got out of his car, checked. The entire bridge had collapsed, and the car ahead had crashed into the river.

We can ask ourselves, "What part of the mind is it that tells us what we need to know?" Scientifically speaking, we have no answer. Metaphysically speaking, we can say there is a soul that knows all and everything—even that a certain bridge is going to collapse. There is an energy at work, and if people are receptive they will be affected by it. They cannot help it.

Communication on a different level is possible among people when they are really bonded and deeply care for each other. Some people will experience this type of communication only in dreams because in the daytime the conscious mind shuts it off. They refuse to accept intuition because of the strong belief in the power of the intellect. The intellect says, "No, it is not possible. There is no proof. There is no evidence." So the message is refused.

But when the message comes in a dream we may pay more attention. The dream creates a certain atmosphere so that it is remembered, and you wake up with a strange kind of feeling, wondering, "Now why would I dream this?" The door is opened a bit more before the intellect steps in and dismisses the experience. Prejudgment is at least delayed. Eventually, if those experiences repeat themselves and prove to be true, the intellect may feel defeated. But if, instead, you always allow the intellect to win, you will lose your most reliable inner guide; and that has to be recognized as your choice.

I have found that men often belittle intuition. I observed that many men who came back from the war told fantastic stories about their extraordinary experiences. Four or five years later they would deny those same stories because their intellect could not understand or explain them. One soldier who was captured in Russia was taken prisoner but managed to escape. There he was in a Russian city where he had never been before, but as he walked down a certain street, he approached a house that he somehow knew was safe—it seemed very familiar to him. He even knew there were twenty-six doors in the house and exactly where the doors were located. He entered the house, and the occupants indeed gave him refuge. When he asked about the doors, he was told, "Yes, there used to be twenty-six doors, but two have been taken off." Several years later the same man denied the whole incident. Personal pride can be a monster that robs you of a treasure.

In our dreams we have to investigate the time element. The reality of the dream may not manifest until years later. Ten years before the Second World War, I had the following dream. I did not pay much attention to dreams at the time because I did not know they could be so important, but this one always came back to mind.

Shrinking Bread and Worn-Out Shoes

I carried a typical German bread basket—the kind that had a handle and was large enough for the big, heavy rye bread. The basket stayed the same size but the bread started to become smaller, until finally it was only a little bun. It looked rather funny in the big basket. And as I walked, I happened to look down at my feet. The beautiful, elegant shoes I was wearing became very crude and so worn out that my toes were sticking out.

That was precisely what happened ten years later. We were so short of food that only a small percentage of the bread was actually grain and the rest was sawdust. Shoes were simply not available. Every scrap of leather was confiscated for the army.

Dreams can give instructions for and solutions to problems that have not yet arisen, as I found out from experience. The war had escalated terribly, and the air raids were intense and frequent. Phosphorous bombs were being dropped on us. When the phosphorous touched the skin, it would spread and burn. One night I had the following dream.

Bandaging the Wounded

A policeman pushed a rather short, stout man toward me. He held out a jar and a number of bandages and said, "Don't just stand there. Help." Then he showed me how to bandage the hand of the man who was all covered with and burning from the phosphorous. I was shown how to anchor the arm, how to put the ointment on with as little rubbing and touching as possible so that the cooling effect of the ointment would work best, and how to bandage and secure every finger.

Some time later there was yet another air raid, and a friend asked me to stay with her because she was very frightened. Even though I had my own place to take care of, I decided to stay with her overnight. On the way home early the next morning, I walked by the park where the bomb shelter I usually went to was located. Stones and rubble were scattered everywhere. A bomb had entirely destroyed the shelter. I stood staring, stunned—overwhelmed by the incredible circumstances that had saved me from death or terrible injury.

Suddenly a policeman pushed a short, stout man toward me. He pushed a jar of ointment into my hand and said, "Don't just stand there. Help." And I did. Staring at the ground to get back the memory of the dream, I applied the ointment onto the man's injured hands without rubbing, and wrapped the bandage around each finger, securing each one as I had been shown.

Receiving these kinds of specific instructions through dreams really opened up my thinking. What is reality? What is a dream? How can a dream present so precisely an event that has not yet occurred? Probably thousands of similar cases are experienced in wars. How does the mind work under intense pressure? In this kind of dramatic circumstance we seem to rely only on that irrational aspect which often prepares us for the next event. A similar situation developed with the following dream.

The Burning House

A house in the neighborhood was burning, and because I was the smallest and the lightest person, I was asked to help. Somebody tied leather belts and ropes around me to hoist me up and lower me into the house, where I threw water onto the fire and put pieces of burning carpets and furniture into the sink.

Later, this incident happened precisely as it had in the dream. I was the smallest person in the shelter so somebody suggested it should be I who was hoisted up using belts and ropes. Because I had seen it in the dream, I had no fear. If it had worked in the dream, I knew it would work now.

As you work with dreams, you will see in due time that this inner guide or inner Guru, inner teacher, inner Light, will respond much more frequently. Then you gain the conviction of its presence. Through observing and classifying your dreams, studying them and following up on what happens in your life, you will reach the point where you can tell when a dream is prophetic.

11

Warning Dreams

HE UNCONSCIOUS MIND through dreams can give us exactly what we need to know—warning us to prepare for the future, warning us about what is or is not good for our physical, emotional, or spiritual well-being, warning us to extend ourselves to help others. It is our responsibility to listen and consciously apply this knowledge to our lives.

For example, a dream of going over a cliff or being close to going over a cliff could mean that you are acting in a way that would bring about the dramatic end of a situation. Is this what you want? If you were going into a business venture and had this dream, it would definitely be telling you not to take the intended action, that it would be just like jumping off a cliff. It is a warning: "Look! You don't know what you're doing!"

Or if in your daily life you have been thinking, "Oh, all these burdens! I'm loaded down with a wife and five little kids, and that's just not what I bargained for. I will leave some finances behind so I can't be accused of being unethical, but I'm going to walk out." Then in your dream you see yourself going off the cliff. The dream is warning you that if you take this action you are symbolically killing yourself, because it will not end where you think it will.

Sometimes even if you feel you are clear about the repercussions of your action, you may not necessarily be so. You may find yourself with an entirely unexpected heart problem, with cancer, or with a broken skull as a result of your action, and if not in this lifetime then in another life. Destiny will not necessarily act through the same channel. You can go to the edge of the fulfillment of your desires, but then your actions based on selfishness and self-will manifest in some results.

"Conscience" is knowing how to discriminate, and if you do not apply awareness when you are able to, your conscience will interfere and warn you. Now you can, of course, silence or overpower your conscience whenever possible. We see that in politics and business all the time. But dreams can bring the message from your conscience that prompts you to ask, "How am I exploiting myself or someone else?"

You have to ask yourself what you are going to do. How will you apply the dream? How will you take action on the warnings you have been given? One woman dreamed as follows.

Five Heavy Suitcases

I saw myself in a train station, preparing to take a trip on my own. But I had five suitcases and nobody to help me with them.

> *When I woke up I had the strong feeling that I really wanted to leave, but I simply didn't know if I could manage the heavy baggage. So I began to think that perhaps I would not go.*

The woman eventually understood the dream to be pointing out her suppressed desire to leave her marriage, and her underlying fear that if she did leave, as she wanted to, she might not be able to take care of the five children, symbolized as the five suitcases (heavy baggage), on her own.

In my work with her I encouraged her to look at the possibility of separation in a straightforward way. How would she be able to manage? I asked her, "What did you do before you were married? Can you revive your career? Or do you want to expand your skills so that you have some means to support your five children?"

She got quite angry at the idea of taking any action. She kept blaming her husband, and she refused to do anything herself to improve her situation or to prepare for a different future. She was not adjusting or surrendering; she was resisting. The dream had given her a warning—will you be able to manage all five on your own? But the woman refused to take action based on the warning, so what could anyone else do? If people are unwilling to help themselves and would rather just complain about how bad their lives are, the situation will not change.

When I came back from my first trip to India, I was not yet aware of dreams in my own life. I did not make a specific effort to remember them, and I did not have a particular method to work with them. But whenever I remembered a dream, I wrote it down. This was one of them.

Protect the Baby!

A baby emerged from my heart. It was so tiny that I could cover it with my hands. Suddenly dark forces appeared in the shape of a dark cloud, which seemed to be after the baby. I knew it and slipped into a big overcoat, holding the baby close to my heart where it was hidden from view. Now I was ready to face whatever came.

What actually happened was that a group of psychologists challenged me. They tried to convince me that, according to their theories, I had chosen spiritual life because of the traumatic events in my life. However, I knew this was absolutely incorrect. I had undergone a spiritual birth[1] in India by accepting my spiritual being and the spiritual aspects of life. By retreating into this new spiritual being in myself, I allowed it to emerge and accepted and acknowledged its presence.

---

[1] The Guru is thought of as a spiritual mother who gives birth to the disciple, the spiritual baby. See *Radha: Diary of a Woman's Search*, for the story of my spiritual birth.

But the dream had warned me that now I must protect it. I needed the extra protection (the large coat) so I could hide the new life which had so recently come into existence. In other words, I was a very new swami and I had to be careful not to talk too openly about spiritual experiences that I had not fully digested myself, precious experiences that could be attacked by the logic and reason of others. By taking refuge in my spiritual being, I found the right answers.

To the psychologists I explained that I had already had certain unusual experiences in my childhood and in my teens that prepared me for what was to happen in India. These events preceded the traumas which they were using for their explanation of the situation. But because those kinds of experiences did not fit into their textbooks, they could not accept them. I said, "I am a canary, but you want me to be a sparrow, like you. However, I am quite happy to be a canary. It is you who cannot tolerate somebody different. It challenges your own security." They were a bit startled, but they did not bother me again for a long time.

The dream had warned me that I would be challenged one day, so I had thought about it beforehand. It is as if you are preparing to travel into new territory—you look at the map and know roughly what route you will take. It may not be precisely what you do, but nevertheless, the preparation prevents some struggle.

At another time I had a different warning dream. In this dream I could hear a rat in the building gnawing at the floor. I thought, "I can hear it, but surely it won't come through because there are at least three or four inches of wood." But the rat kept gnawing at the wood, obviously not giving up. I had to look around in my waking life to see if someone was undermining the foundation of the spiritual work, because that, to me, was the message. I may have been accepting someone in good faith when I should not have done so. What would "undermining" mean? In this case it meant acting or living contrary to the ideals of the ashram. There is no sense in anyone living in a spiritual community who does not share its ideals. When I had the confirmation, I could take action.

~

You can also have warning dreams about health and food: "Don't eat this," or "That is poison."

One of the young men at the ashram was a real chocolate lover. I worried about his health, but I did not want to act like his mother, so I kept silent. Once, when he was doing some carpentry in a small store and the shopkeeper mentioned that his chocolate was all outdated and would have to be thrown out, the young man asked if he could take it home. For the next week he ate only chocolate and not a single meal. Then he had a dream. He went into a store to buy a chocolate bar, and the usual price was crossed out. Instead, there was a big red sticker with a new and higher price. Did that mean that chocolate bars would become more expensive? No. Why should his unconscious worry about that? The message was that the chocolate bars were becoming more expensive for his health.

Dreams can be very direct and practical. When pizza first became popular I decided to try it, too, just for the change and to join in the fun. I ate it once. That night I had a dream.

Not Good For You!

There was a nice, big pizza on some sort of a board. A big hand came, pulled it away, and said, "Not good for you!"

Of course I paid attention to the dream and never ate pizza again. The dream also helped me to understand that I should look after my physical well-being. I used to be quite critical of my own Guru—he could not eat this and he could not eat that, and I wondered, "What's the point of yogic practice if it creates all these limitations?" What I did not understand at the time was that the increased spiritual practice creates a heightened sensitivity in the cells of the body.

But could the message of my dream, besides referring to my health and physical well-being, also have been symbolic? Yes, it could have been. For example, if I had been a young lady with an Italian boyfriend, the dream might have warned me that "this Italian stuff" was not the right thing for me!

Another member of the ashram dreamed he had marvelous sandwiches with tomatoes and lettuce and all kinds of vegetables fresh from the garden. In the dream he threw the food into the outhouse. I suggested that this was a sign either that his digestive system did not make use of the physical food he was eating, or that he was rejecting the nourishment he received spiritually. I asked him if he was throwing out what was good for him and letting his emotional needs and desires run his life.

Actually both interpretations went hand in hand, because the understanding on a gross level often invites investigation on a more refined level. The food was the gross level and his body, indeed, did not digest it well. But it was also true that he did not digest the teachings well. So sometimes a dream that seems to be about health will also have a different meaning.

I always ask, "What do you feed your body? Now tell me, what do you feed your mind?"

A very successful businessman in the Midwest was quite sick with cancer. He was already bedridden when I saw him, but he had a stack of terrible books on his night table. I said, "You must realize that your days are numbered. Is that what you want to take with you—this junk?"

What do you feed your mind? If you do not feed your mind good and healthy food, what do you expect? Discrimination and self-control are really the keys. We cannot live without them. You cannot become anything unless you work at it. We understand this principle in general life, but many people seem to refuse to accept it when it comes to spiritual life and growing beyond their self-created limitations. And sometimes a life is wasted by the attitude that says, "I don't need to do that." No, you do not—you need to do it only if you want to achieve something in your life.

I needed no further interpretation for the following dream.

Share, Share, Share!

I had a perfectly well-balanced meal—what might be called "scientifically nutritious." I had found a formula for preparing and eating the foods, and I was going to keep this to myself. Suddenly a voice in my dream said, "Share, share, share! You must share as you go along."

When you become aware that dreams can give you warnings and when you act on their warnings, you can save yourself from sometimes costly mistakes and wrong actions. In this way, you cooperate with your unconscious.

12

Dream Sharing

*I*T IS VERY difficult for most people to understand the oneness that all spiritual teachers talk about. And there is no easy way to learn about this oneness except by experiencing the interaction of minds.

I remember a conversation I had with one woman about the interaction of minds. Her husband was leaving her for a younger woman, so in her own mind she pleaded with him to stay and offered him her heart. But it had no effect. She said to me, "If you think my mind could influence his, you're wrong. It doesn't work." But in this case it was her motivation that was wrong. She was not motivated to understand the interconnection of minds, but simply wanted to force her husband to come back by the power of her will. Unfortunately he had been under the power of her will throughout their marriage, so it was the very force he was trying to escape.

But if somebody sincerely attempts to understand the functioning of the mind beyond the ordinary and really tries to discover if there is truth to it, something can happen. When two people are open to each other and neither is dominating any aspect of the other's life, they can experience a truly beautiful communication. This communication is usually known only between Gurus and disciples, and only when the disciple is able and willing to receive. Much of what I learned from my Guru, Swami Sivananda, was beyond words. He would sometimes ask the swamis to bring a huge pillow for me so I could sit beside him at Satsang. He would say, "Sit here on this side"—which was his left side—"and cover your face so people won't stare at you." Then as I stilled my mind there would be a flow of energy, and I would receive knowledge of very intricate teachings much more clearly than through any words he could have used.

Sometimes if a dream group works closely together for a long time, several members may have a similar dream at the same time, or even dream parts of the same dream. Watch for this and think about the interplay of minds, or the oneness it indicates. In my dream work with students at the ashram, I sometimes dreamed the other half of their dream, to their astonishment and sometimes shock. This phenomenon of one person dreaming a part of another's dream is what I mean by

"dream sharing" or "mutual dreaming." Here is an example of one case.

We once had a rabbi living at the ashram. A few months before this young man was to be ordained a rabbi, he realized he knew how to perform the rituals and how to present the doctrines; he knew how to speak Hebrew and ancient Hebrew. But his academic training was not teaching him how to comfort people on their deathbeds or how to answer questions about faith and belief. It did not strengthen his own spiritual quest. When he expressed his predicament to another rabbi, who happened to know me, this man suggested, "When you finish your training, go for a year to Swami Radha's ashram in the mountains."

"What can I do as a rabbi at an ashram in the mountains?" asked the young man.

The rabbi said, "Don't worry. She won't try to convert you. But you will find what you need."

So he came. What I did was give him the yogic practices and ask him to find the corresponding words and ideas in his own religious tradition: "Translate OM into its equivalent from your religion. Chant the Mantra using *Elohim* instead of *Hari Om*."[1]

According to Jewish tradition there is no image of God, even though the text speaks of "him," and "the Lord," and "he," all implying an image. So in many ways it was not very easy for the young rabbi to understand Eastern symbolism. But when it came to exploring the mind, he had an extremely good understanding. And he worked with me on his dreams. Several times he came

---

[1] See Swami Sivananda Radha, *Mantras: Words of Power,* rev. ed. (Spokane, Wash.: Timeless Books, 1994).

and said, "I didn't have a dream," or sometimes, "I didn't bring a dream." At first I did not notice the important difference in how he said this.

One day I asked him, "Have you ever had dreams that pointed to the interconnection of minds, or dreams that took you beyond the psychological level?"

He said that although there was a mystical branch of Judaism, he himself had never had that kind of experience.

One night I had gone to bed very tired but woke up after two hours. I wondered why I could not sleep and if I should perhaps take a bath to relax. While I was thinking about it, I remembered a voice from my dream saying, "Bobbe, Bobbe." But the next morning I did not recall it.

A few days later at six o'clock in the morning I was in the office preparing the mailing by sticking the address labels and stamps onto the newsletters. I checked all the addresses and was sorting them out by states and provinces. While I was busy with this, suddenly I heard a voice saying, "Bobbe, Bobbe." I looked around and did not see anybody in the room. I thought, "Well, all right then, somebody is going to come in soon. Don't pay any attention to it." I was sticking on the stamps, sorting letters, putting elastics around the bundles. My mind was at that moment only slightly occupied with this very undemanding mental activity.

Then I heard the voice again, "Bobbe, Bobbe," but this time it went on a little longer. Suddenly I remembered the dream. I was not asleep now, but this was the same voice I had heard in my dream calling again, "Bobbe, Bobbe." And now the voice said, "Go and wake up Jerry. Tell him I'm here." (Jerry was the rabbi.) Still believing that there must be a person somewhere in the kitchen or in the other part of the house, I said, "Jerry's still in bed."

"Well, go and get him!"

I thought this was very strange. I looked around. There was nobody there! It was only six o'clock in the morning. Everybody had been busy digging ditches for the disposal fields, so they must have been sleeping like big, heavy logs. I realized something else must be happening. I sat and thought, "Is this a dream?" Sometimes I see something but do not hear anything. Now I hear something but do not see anything. What is the state of mind that can produce voices? What was this voice? Where did it come from? I wanted to know.

By eight o'clock everybody slowly tumbled into the house for breakfast, Jerry among them. I immediately asked him, "Jerry, who is Bobbe?" Before he answered, I carried on to tell him why I wanted to know. "First the voice came in a dream. Then, just this morning there was somebody here saying, 'Bobbe, Bobbe,' and, 'Go and wake up Jerry.' Any idea what that means? This morning I was not asleep. I was working here at the table with the ashram newsletter."

Jerry stood there as if he were glued to the ground, his face turning white as a ghost. Finally he sat down and looked at me and asked, "Can you say that again?"

So I repeated the whole story.

Then he said, "I had a dream that I didn't want to bring to class because I did not want to think about it. In fact, I had several dreams I did not want to discuss. I did not want to know. But now if it spills over to you, I guess I will have to look at them." He said he had dreamed of his grandmother, whom Jewish children call "Bobbe." And she told him that she had guided his steps here.

He asked her, "How can you do this? I remember you from when I was a little boy of four or five, and you used to tell me stories while I sat on your lap. But you've been dead for a long time."

She said, "No, that's a mistake. I am not really dead. I am very alive. Once again I tell you that I guided your steps to come here. I know precisely what you are doing and where you are, and I support you with my prayers."

Now Jerry admitted, "I didn't want to think about what this implied, so I did not bring the dream to class." It challenged some underlying convictions.

The interaction between Jerry and myself was an interplay of forces in which my help was enlisted much more intensely than usual to bring a point across and to penetrate certain concepts. His dreams combined with my dream and experience helped him to reassess. He began to gain a personal understanding that there is no final end to anything, that everything is in flux. Everything changes—sometimes very quickly, sometimes very slowly indeed—too slowly even to be observed in one lifetime.

~

I had a different experience of dream sharing when another woman received an important message for me through a dream. The message was that my Guru, Swami Sivananda, would be leaving the earth. Probably the dream would have been too upsetting to me or perhaps I would have perceived it almost as a rejection, so this dream was dreamed by someone else and brought to me. The woman who dreamed it said, "I'm sure it's your dream, Swami Radha. I have never met Swami Sivananda and I've seen him only in pictures with you. In the dream he said, 'Tell Radha I give her back the coat she brought to me. I will have no need of it.'" The coat was one of my gifts to him when I first went to India.

On each of the three nights preceding this woman's phone call, I had awakened at three o'clock in the morning hearing, "Sivananda, Sivananda." I did not know what to make of it and felt very disturbed. I was staying at a friend's house, and she commented, "My goodness, can't you smile? I thought spiritual people were always happy." By the end of the week the phone call came, which brought a clear message soon to be confirmed by my Guru's passing.

Experiences like these lead us to ask, "What is the mind? And where does one mind end and another begin?"

13

Past Lives & Dreams

IF YOU WANT to go to the recesses of the unconscious and explore the possibility of past lives, you first have to clarify why you would want to know. Why is it so important? If you think that the knowledge would help you to understand a particular weakness or to develop a needed strength in your present life, you may be given that information through a dream. But influences from past lives can only be taken as a possibility, and then only if they aid you in what you are trying to achieve in this life. It would be foolish to use something that does not help, and it is entirely up to you how far you want to explore this area.

Suppose you are a very successful lawyer, but in another life you were a monk or nun. The karmic influence from your monastic life might now prevent you from feeling really happy with your present success. People may think you are very lucky because you have respect, financial success, and perhaps a beautiful family. Yet you may feel that there must be more to life than that, and then wonder why you have such strange thoughts. If the soul wants to fulfill its commitment to the Most High, of course you will not be happy, no matter how high your career goes or how much money you make. There will always be something missing. When you find out that something is missing and go in search of it, influences from the distant past may come back. Even the fact that you do not know how this works or cannot prove it is not important. What is important is to find out what this lifetime is all about. Can you find the purpose of your life? If you discover that the purpose of your life is to attain Self-Realization—even if you cannot quite believe it and even if you cannot explain what the driving force behind it is—still you may have enough curiosity and perseverance to go on.

The conscious mind will run in circles until logic and reason are exhausted and something else—intuitive perception—takes over. Then, in due time, the answer may arise. Forgotten fragments can surface in dreams. As you put each little piece of the mosaic together, suddenly a larger picture may emerge. Patches may be left that are never quite complete, but you may see enough to recognize the picture and to gain a greater understanding of yourself.

The past may appear in a condensed version in the dream and reveal something of great importance for your further development. It may not be important whether or not the dream is a perfect recollection from a former life, as long as you get the message.

But if you do not have the intense urge to know and understand, there is no point in pursuing memories. Because with the emergence of the past comes the recognition of past mistakes. You have to consider and accept that you may not have been so great in the past. Perhaps you were unfaithful and left the spiritual path. Perhaps you were disloyal to the pursuit of the purpose of your life. Then the dream—through the setting, the century, and the nationality—may give you a bit of a shock to help you realize that you need to hurry up, that you cannot really afford to waste time, that you must do everything possible in this lifetime.

No one has to accept reincarnation, but the theory seems reasonable. You can always take the opposite viewpoint, that there is no purpose in life, that we are like apples that will eventually fall from the tree and rot. But if you start to ask, "What else is there?" the unconscious may suddenly speak up through a dream. Perhaps in the dream you will be standing in front of a mirror combing your hair, and you see a different face looking back. While you are looking and questioning, "What is this?" the whole thing blurs, and still another face appears. Then after a while you can watch this whole performance with great amusement, or anticipation and curiosity, not realizing that what you are seeing is basically always the same face. It is you. You can ask yourself, "What is my original face?" and pursue the question until you have the experience of it.

When you have a dream that you think might refer to a past life, first look at how the dream can apply to your life right now. Here is how I worked with one such dream.

The Herb Healer

A voice said, "You were once an Indian, called by the people, the Herb Healer." I knew I was in a male body and was a member of the tribe that lived at the bottom of the Grand Canyon. The voice also said, "You had the knowledge of how to heal every illness, because for every illness there is an herb." I saw that there was a document which showed the herbs for all illnesses. On the cover was a bird on the left side and a five-pointed leaf on the right.

Was this a dream of a past life? How would I know? Before I jumped into that line of thought, I decided to look at how I could apply the dream right here and now. What do I know about herbs, and can I use that knowledge now? During the war, when there was no medicine, we went back to home remedies of earlier times. Many remedies that I had learned from my grandmother had proven very useful. Maybe I could recover those and the knowledge of plants she had passed on to me.

So I went around the grounds of the ashram discovering which of the different plants I could remember and the purpose for which they were used—clover, dandelion, certain types of thistles. Then I gathered together all the edible wild greens I knew and presented the ashram with a new type of salad.

What else could I do? Make a list of herbs? Take pictures and identify them? Research their botanical names? And once I had this all together, should I give it to people or make it into a booklet? I started by studying any books I could find on the subject, researching and collecting information.

Around this time the previous owner of the property came to see us, looking very miserable. He had a terrible sinus condition and was scheduled for an operation in two weeks. This poor man was very fearful. Could I do anything to help him? When I asked if he would like to try an herbal treatment, he was very eager to try anything that might help. I told him how to prepare an ointment in a manner that I remembered. As it turned out, his condition improved so much that he did not need the operation. So I could see there were benefits from recovering what I knew about herbs, even if I did not conclude that the dream referred to a past life.

Some time later I was invited to Phoenix, Arizona, by some friends. I casually tried to find out if they knew anything about Indians living at the bottom of the Grand Canyon. My friends, having known me for quite some time, became suspicious that I wanted to know something specific for specific reasons.

The woman went to town and came back a few hours later with a local magazine that just happened to feature a story on the Havasupai Indians who live at the bottom of the Grand Canyon. When she gave me the magazine, I could not open it. Everything in me was on alert—every hair on my body standing on end. I said a polite thank you and kept the magazine for a long time before opening it. I just did not want to know, at first. If it were true, what would it mean? The fact that my friend had found the magazine and instantly confirmed the possibility that my dream could have had a reality in the past is an example of what I call "substantiation."[1]

Finally I read the story. It said the tribe is still two hundred strong and that they live in a place where the Canyon forms a wider valley. Not more than two hundred people could survive there.

For a long time I found this a very unpleasant, irritating, and confusing position to be in—dreaming about a past life and so quickly finding an indication of a basis in reality. What about my other dreams? Did all my other dreams have a much greater reality than I had given them? Would I have to revise the interpretations of all my dreams? Read and study them all again? So I did. I worked my way through, starting at the beginning and coming forward. I could see the incredible resources my dreams had given me and how many messages I had missed on quite a different level. It was a tremendous revelation.

So it might be possible to have dreams that refer to past lives. But because we live in the here and now, such dreams should only be pursued in order to find out what is left from that particular lifetime for us to learn now. Some dreams may be only reminders, with no other weight than to say, "Yes, you have had many lifetimes"— almost an assurance that, "Yes, if you can't make it in

---

[1] See chapter 27 "Substantiation of Spiritual Dreams," pages 301-311.

this lifetime, you will be given more." But put all your effort into evolving, because each life delays. And each delay is quite painful, as you go through the human experience over and over again.

When I was in Mexico, I had the following dream after visiting several ruins.

Jubal and Incal

I saw a very old house that looked like an old ruin, walls torn down, piles of stones lying around. It was very rough, but one part still seemed to be complete. I was standing near an entrance covered with cloth when an old woman appeared. She asked me in a very sharp voice, "What do you want?"

I said, "I am looking for two people—Jubal and Incal."

She was rather short with me: "I have lived here all my life, and whoever they are, I don't know them. It must have been a long time ago," she said. "They must have been dead for a long time."

Curiosity is not always a good thing, so after this dream I did not even make an attempt to find out how I came upon these two names, even though they had come in a dream. Could some dreams just indicate that we have lived in this or that culture at one point? Perhaps we are drawn back there to trace our lives. But then you have to think, "I may have lived there at that time and my old body may even be buried there, but it is like a dress I have taken off. Why would I want to put it on again?" Let the past be the past, or as Jesus said, "Let the dead bury the dead."[2]

---

[2] Luke 9:60

Some dreams may indicate a resolution of past lives. Perhaps you see yourself in an interaction with another person, and then see accounts that show a zero balance. It could mean the karmic debts that had linked the two of you in the past have been paid off.

Or perhaps you find yourself embracing many different people from different cultures, as I did in the following dream.

Embracing All

I was welcoming many different types of people into a round ceremonial building. Each person was wearing clothing from different cultures around the world. Some were very strangely dressed in a way I had never seen in any existing culture today. Each person came to me and we embraced warmly.

Perhaps these were all my personality aspects. If this was so, I was quite satisfied because it meant I had integrated all of them. But if, in fact, the dream was referring to past lives and suggesting I had lived in each of these cultures at various times, I also had no regrets because I welcomed each of them.

Dreams such as these stimulate questions. As long as we do not have definite answers for such occurrences, we can at least allow the mind to exercise itself, considering all possibilities in order to become flexible and workable. When you study your dream symbols you will see how the unconscious presents details and information in a way that is acceptable to you, because the Higher Consciousness uses the language that comes from yourself.

14

Dreams of Spiritual Guidance

YOUR DREAMS WILL guide you if you are willing to receive their guidance. Your willingness can arise either from understanding and using your intelligence properly or from desperation, when you are in so much trouble or pain that listening to your Higher Self is your only recourse. You can learn by cooperating with the Divine or you can learn by being forced into it, like an alcoholic who will not give up his bottle until he has almost destroyed his human dignity. But then you bring the law of karma upon yourself. It is up to you. Do you want to learn the hard way? If you do not want to listen to yourself there is nothing much anyone else can do. You have to become more desperate, feel more pain.

But if you can listen to yourself, the guidance from the unconscious through dreams will be extremely valuable. The directions for which spiritual path you should follow can be given to you by your own Higher Self in a dream or a series of dreams. Different people will have different experiences. If you dream of going through seven gates, you might well understand that the path of Kundalini is most suitable for you. If you dream you are walking through a park and suddenly see an image of the Buddha or Tara, perhaps Buddhism is your path. Were the features Japanese, Thai, Tibetan, or Indian? Fritjof Capra dreamed that the subatomic world was Lord Siva's dance, and with that he united his background in physics with his understanding of Eastern philosophy.[1] If you dream of Divine Mother dancing the dance of creation or continuous manifestation, then yours is probably the path of devotion to the divine feminine.

There is no one way that is right for everybody. But there is one particular way for you, which is the best way for you get to know yourself, the best way for you to cooperate with your spiritual growth. That way can be shown to you through dreams.

Dreams will reassure you that you are on the right path. Dreams may also comfort you when you feel desperate, when you think, "Why can't I learn more quickly? Why does it take so long?" Dreams can show you precisely your own process of growth.

---

[1] Fritjof Capra, *The Tao of Physics* (Boston: Shambhala Publications, 1975).

When I returned to North America from my first trip to India, I felt I had so much to learn and I wondered if I would ever make any progress. I asked myself, "When will I really flower into this great conscious being? How can I achieve Self-Realization? It is probably not possible. It must be a fairy tale from long ago, a creation of the mind based on the human desire for perfection."

During this time of struggle I had the following dream.

The Golden Flower of Consciousness

A tiny seed, so small it looked like a speck of dust, was starting to take root. It was as if I had X-ray eyes and I could clearly see these roots—white, spreading, a whole network. Then a tiny shoot came forth and slowly, slowly began to grow. Then a bud formed, hiding what was inside, and gradually opened into two very coarse leaves. After what seemed an eternity the shoot continued growing upwards. Then another bud formed, and leaves—this time a little finer—unfolded. The shoot slowly kept growing and growing until another pair of leaves unfolded, even finer in their structure.

Again and again the sprout would grow, and each time the pair of leaves that opened was a little finer than the last. At last a different kind of bud began to grow, one that had many tiny leaves. As this large bud slowly began to unfold, the rest of the plant almost disappeared but was lit up from the inside. And I looked into an exquisite golden flower—the Golden Flower of Consciousness.

This experience prompted me to take great care in the study of Kundalini Yoga, whose crown is the thousand-petaled lotus. The flower in my vision or dream was similar to the lotus although not exactly the same. Obviously, however, it represented metamorphosis and it gave me a clear message.

If another person, even another yogi, had suggested to me, "Why don't you follow the path of Kundalini?" I would have thought, "Yes, maybe. But how will I know for sure that it is right for me?" When my own Higher Self showed me in such a vivid demonstration, I had no doubts, because what developed and emerged had come out of myself. That which naturally emerged and unfolded out of myself I could not doubt. But even if I had doubted it, at least I would have been led to test it. And then I would know.

Your dreams will also show you when you should do some actual worship. They will take you to a temple, to a cathedral; they will show you incredible images, which may finally vanish in the sky or become enormous. You may have spiritual dreams, which are milestones on the Royal Highway. You may dream so clearly that you have a little metal Buddha in your pocket that the next day you check and ask yourself, "Do I have a Buddha here or do I not? Did somebody put it into my pocket and I just didn't notice it earlier?" In other words you receive messages that the Divine has become closer in whichever way you can understand it.

~

Can you find your Guru through a dream? There are many stories in the Orient of seekers doing so. But to find your Guru through a dream, you must be in a state

of urgency, a state of intense homesickness for your spiritual home. Unless this urgency is present, the meeting with the Guru cannot take place. Sometimes you may have a dream image that shows you the next step for your spiritual development. But even then it is difficult to know if the image is referring to an actual person, or if it is a symbol that you can accept for your Higher Self.

If you really want to come close to the Divine, your intensity will make you receptive to someone who can respond to your call. It is possible that the Guru will project himself or herself onto the receptive mind of the disciple, particularly if there has been a relationship in previous births. If your intensity and sincerity allow it, meeting the Guru this way, in the heart, has an even greater reality than meeting him or her in the physical body.

If the intensity and receptivity are present to an extraordinary degree, even initiation can take place in a dream. But if the person seeking initiation is far from being able to fulfill the requirements of "fitting into" his or her body of Light,[2] the teacher will know that the time is not right and there can be no initiation, either in a dream or in the waking state.

If you are already in a relationship with a Guru and the Guru appears in your dreams, you have to question what the image signifies. Is it an actual projection of the Guru's presence to bring you an important message? Is it an image of your Higher Self? Or is it a symbol for

---

[2] "Fitting into the body of Light" means being willing to let go of identification with the body and mind, and instead identifying with the essential spiritual nature, symbolized as Light.

your own conscience? Be very clear about how you interpret it and watch that you do not interpret according to your convenience.

For example, if you have a dream where the teacher is watching over you in a judgmental sort of way, you have probably turned the Guru into some kind of policeman or policewoman in your own mind, someone who has to act as your conscience in a rather negative way. You can then justify yourself in your own mind and triumphantly think, "See! My Higher Self is showing me that my Guru is really just trying to find fault with me." You might also learn where your conscience is troubled. So your dream reveals your own thinking and reflects your relationship with the Guru, giving you the chance to ask if this is the way you want the relationship to be.

I do not accept that the Guru is continuously with the disciple and that the voice of wisdom is always the Guru's, as is commonly taught in India. I could recognize Swami Sivananda's voice by his very distinct way of speaking, his particular pitch and tone, his Indian English. When it was my own English, I understood that the message may be from my Higher Self. When you can really listen in daily life, you can also hear in a dream, and then you will be able to distinguish the voice of the Guru in your dreams.

This Way!

A thundering voice called to me, "Radha! That's enough now. Come out!" I was just in a big swimming pool having fun, being with many people. No sinful action. "This way!" he said.

It was very typical of my Guru's voice and his way of speaking. Swami Sivananda did not use many words, and they were very short and direct. That was it. I knew the message was from him, and I understood what the message was. I was not supposed to complete the academic program I had entered. I was not supposed to play in that pool, enjoying the fun. My Guru had other work for me to do and I could not be distracted.

Similarly, if you do not know which Mantra is the best for you,[3] your unconscious may present it to you in a dream once your emotional problems have been cleared away. You may hear the melody in your sleep and learn just how the Mantra is to be chanted.

We are given lots of help if we just look for it. If you are sincere and receptive in your work with dreams, you will discover the extraordinary instructions and guidance they can bring.

---

[3] There is said to be a specific Mantra for each person, called their Ishta Mantra. See Radha, *Mantras*, 16.

15

Levels of Dreams

S YOU PRACTICE watching dreams, analyzing them, and learning the language of your unconscious, you will begin to observe the different levels in dreams. Many levels can be reflected in dreams: the physical, the psychological, the emotional—ranging from fear to delight; all five senses can be reflected, and so can your faith and intensity of desire for the Divine. Dreams show you just where you are. It is like looking into a mirror.

But it is very wise to interpret dreams first on the level of everyday existence, and only then to see if the dream has a higher meaning and to make the great effort to lift the mind up to that level. When your dreams also apply to a higher level, you can be quite sure that your development is taking place gently, but smoothly and steadily. This is usually better than developing in jumps and spurts and then going backwards.

How do you know when it is time to start working with your dreams as more than psychological reflections? If you can see the dream in a different way, interpret it that way. Explore as much as possible, because a dream may have meaning on several levels at once. On one level, the level of daily living—Yes, the window needs to be cleaned. I couldn't see out the window because it was dirty. On another level—Do I not have a clear vision of my potential? What filters am I putting on? What is my vision of the Divine? What do I faintly perceive?

There are many levels of meaning that must be recognized simultaneously because they tell you that there are successive stages of development available to you. We can elevate the symbolic language in which our unconscious speaks to us and in this way learn how the inner being expresses itself.

When the messages of many dreams are put together, a "super message" may suddenly emerge. You can then see all your messages as milestones, and you can tell where you have moved forward and where you have not. You can see when your dreams implied only suppressed daily living concerns, and which psychological obstacles have to be removed to allow the spiritual aspects to come through.

However, you have to realize that whatever level the dream is at, it still comes from you. If the voice of the "you" that speaks through dreams is not clear, some part of you is not ready to get it clear. Talking about "levels" could be misleading if you take it to imply hierarchy and adopt a judgmental attitude, thinking you yourself must be either "high-level" or "low-level." Judgment is to be avoided in working with dreams. When you talk about levels, you must still understand that "you are all one." Think of the physical being—we have the skeletal system, the muscular system, the circulatory system, the digestive system, but we would not necessarily identify with only one system. They all function together. There is an interplay of forces that deals with and organizes our physical existence. In the same way, we cannot completely separate psychological dreams from spiritual ones. Neither can we totally separate the human from the Divine.

What is human and what is Divine? What is the ego? The ego is more than vanity, pride, or self-importance, which are just its characteristics. The ego is the tremendous force that holds together our physical bodies and all our cells. The ego is also the force that ties together our personality aspects. If you are really serious and pull out one personality aspect, the whole personality aspect structure will become a little looser. In other words, if you work on your major shortcomings, you do not need to worry about many other aspects. They will just fall away.

The ego has its own reality. The world in which we live our daily lives has a reality of its own, but it must not overlie the reality of our spiritual being. If you say, "I cannot be spiritual because it doesn't fit into my successful life," that is not accurate. Your successes are not your own. Without the support and help of the Divine, you would have no victories whatsoever. It takes a great deal of awareness to recognize that.

The ego is also part of the essence of our own divinity. The essence of the eternal is to be found in any human being who wants to tune in to it. It is only a matter of quantity. A drop of water from the ocean is not the whole ocean, but it has the same essence. It is important to know the deep in the drop as well as the deep in the ocean. When you put the drop back into the ocean, you will never find it again. If you insist on your individuality, the ultimate union—merging with the Divine—will never take place. It cannot.

The human is a vehicle for the expression of the Divine. If we, as individuals, are indeed part of God, we also inhabit God and God lives within us. The kingdom of God is within. There is no way that we can have Cosmic Love, even to a small degree, unless it comes from that original source of Cosmic Love.

The essence in you is always there. It may appear lost for many lifetimes, but you are always a unit, having one aspect that is human and one aspect that is divine, and the two aspects have to come together. That complete unit is part of a greater whole. One drop of the ocean is still part of the ocean; it does not become something different. The waves of the ocean are not different from the ocean.

I had a dream many years ago that presented this idea in a simple, but unusual way.

The Brown and the Blue Shoe

One of the young men from the ashram came home with a box that had only one shoe in it. When I suggested he

go back to the store to pick up the missing shoe, he felt uncomfortable about it and asked me if I would go instead. I looked carefully at the shoe and then went. The clerk was a bit embarrassed but set off to look for the missing shoe. When he came back he told me that it was not in the store and suggested I go to the manager's house. He gave me directions.

The manager had a well-organized storeroom, but he searched for quite a while before finding the second shoe, which was somewhat hidden on the top shelf. I thanked him and returned home. When we compared the two shoes we found they were exactly alike except for one big difference: the shoe the young man already had was brown, and the one I brought back was blue. He said he could not possibly wear shoes of two different colors. He asked me, "Please go again and try to find two shoes of the same color."

This time the manager made no attempt even to look for another shoe. He said with a smile, "Go back and think about it—we walk with one foot on the brown path and the other on the blue." As I walked home I looked down at my own shoes and realized that I, too, walked in shoes of different colors: one for the brown path of the earth—the physical world, the other for the blue path of the sky—the spiritual world.

The dream emphasized the coexistence of the physical and the spiritual. When that coexistence is in balance, we have harmony. However, to achieve this harmony you have to go beyond the fear of criticism because otherwise you will not dare to think of yourself as Divine. But if you do not accept the Divine in yourself, you cannot accept it in others. If you never accept the Divine in yourself, you deny the Divine. That is the crucifixion within. You crucify the Divine, by denying it. What is necessary, instead, is to crucify the ego. If you can do that, your dream will be on the level of direct contact with the Divine.

∿

As you work with understanding the many layers within yourself, you may find out that your dream also has many layers. It may give you psychological information about what you are doing or what you should do, but it may also give you instructions on a different level, a spiritual level. However, if a dream carries a message on an even more basic level, we must not ignore that. We are what we are, and we have to deal with all aspects of ourselves.

Suppose you have a dream in which you see a beautiful orchid. How would you classify this dream? On which level is it, and how would you determine that? Perhaps you would start to look at the dream from a purely psychological standpoint. You might notice that the flower is very delicate and the leaves are as stiff as leather. Does that indicate a certain sensitivity amid a certain coarseness? Perhaps you interpret it to mean that you have both qualities. Then you may ask, "What am I sensitive to? To my pride? To my vanity? What is the purpose of the coarseness? To protect that sensitivity?"

But is it only that? Although you may arrive at a good understanding at this level, you do not want to limit yourself to these aspects and miss another message. You can explore further. If I take the coarse leaves as my human nature—yes, that is there. But can the flower be something else besides a symbol of my pride? Is there something flowering within me? If it takes seven years for an orchid to flower, maybe I need to persist in order to allow my spiritual unfolding.

You may know that an orchid perches high up in the trees but lives only on water and air, not taking anything from the tree itself, and that according to botanists, the orchid is the most highly developed of all flowers. So when you interpret the dream you may think, "It would be wonderful if I could subsist on such simplicity—looking after my physical being, as symbolized by the water, and being sustained by a spiritual atmosphere, symbolized by the air; only these two elements, not a whole range of delicacies and desires. But still the leaves are firm and strong."

You can take this one dream and make it a masterpiece of investigation. You might find out where orchids grow. There are many types of orchids. Which one was it? Can you identify something similar? What was the color? Was it the type that grows in the ground? Was it one of the wild orchids that are protected by law and cannot be transplanted? Perhaps this refers not to a literal transplanting or moving to a new city or country, but to your thinking—the city of your being, the city of your life. In Indian terms, you create your three worlds (the past, the present, and the future). Because you have the power to create them, you can withdraw that power; you can destroy your three worlds. When the three worlds collapse, you enter eternal life or your inner Light whose energy can never be destroyed.

When you have understood the dream in as many different ways as you can, you might reflect more on your spiritual flowering. The idea might entice you. You may not believe that this spiritual flowering could take place, but the dream is saying it is a possibility. Your human nature might stand in the way and say, "No, you're not good enough. Be reasonable—it's just your pride and your vanity wanting to be somebody special." But if in your waking state, you can see the spiritual flowering level of the dream, then you must recognize that if you were not on your way, you would not even see it. If you were not on your way to San Francisco, you would not find the Golden Gate Bridge.

Eventually you may be able to relate every bit of your dream to different events in your life and put them all together. But sometimes, no matter how careful you are, you may miss one aspect because your concept of yourself is too low for you even to consider the possibility. Some people who are very self-critical often miss what I call "a divine message" in a dream. There can indeed be a very beautiful message, a short projection of what your life might be. It is wonderful to see how the unconscious tries to get the message through. It is very helpful if you can accept it. Whatever you think about yourself, try to look at all the possibilities because we often have some strange ideas that limit our potential.

If you have investigated many dreams, and if you have worked intensely on your personal problems in order to overcome your weaknesses and shortcomings, you may experience dreams that lead you to understand that your life is not any different from a dream. If you want to change your life, you can change it—not very easily, however, because intellect and reasoning, the processes that helped you to survive to this point, will not let go so easily. But clear dreams can be the message to attempt it—now—not in a year or two.

We can develop to the point where certain dreams become more real to us than daily life. We know there is a certain reality in making our meals, in caring for our homes, and in our daily living concerns—and we can see that as one level of reality. But if we have a dream, as one great yogi did,[1] that Liberation is possible in one lifetime, naturally such a dream is a very rare experience. It belongs on a very different level and has a much greater value.

As you work with the various levels of a dream, you may begin to realize that you, the dreamer, know better than you, the daydreamer. The daydreamer may still be caught in worldly pursuits, but the dreamer may already have decided, "What is the point?" The dreamer may already be on the path to the Light.

---

[1] W. J. Evans-Wentz, ed. *Tibet's Great Yogi: Milarepa.* 2d ed. (London: Oxford University Press, 1969).

16

An Expanded Method

W *HERE IS GOD? Why do you think there is a God? How do you know? Where does God reside? When you pray, how do you know that your prayer will go to God? Can God listen? Why would God listen? Are you so important that God should pay attention? And how does your prayer get there? How do you know the Guru? Is it a matter of time? Length of prayers? How long will it take you to find God? To find the Guru?*

This kind of battery of rapid, non-stop questions was an experience I underwent with my Tibetan Guru. He would choose four significant words—for example,

God, Guru, prayer, and *time*—and constantly throw them back and forth in a bombardment of questions.[1] I found that this method shattered many of my deep-rooted opinions and set me free from concepts that I had accepted without investigation. We have created our own mental prisons with false beliefs, misunderstandings, and cultural and social conditioning. This type of questioning speeds up the development of awareness by diminishing the ideas and concepts that hold us prisoners.

Once you are well-established in the process of interpreting dreams given in the Methods chapter, you can move on to an advanced technique based on this same idea of rapid self-questioning. This method will help you delve further into the meaning of different words and their combinations. You can begin to break up false beliefs, strong opinions, and deeply ingrained ideas that have come from your past conditioning.

I have found that when people work with the symbols from their dreams, they often list a whole string of other words as their associations. To break this Western habit of conceptualizing without sufficient investigation, the instructions for this approach are to treat every word in your list of associations as a key word or phrase and investigate it, through rapid-fire questioning, in relation to every other association.

This method is very good for going into depth, connecting you to something within yourself, and eventually to the Divine. You may want to tape your questions,

---

[1] See Swami Sivananda Radha, *In the Company of the Wise* (Spokane, Wash.: Timeless Books, 1991), 33-41.

because writing takes longer and you want your thoughts to arise quickly. This spontaneity can help a great deal. The process I am suggesting here for your dreams is not quite as dramatic as the Tibetan Guru's approach. With your dreams you are at least using your own words which you already have on paper. They are familiar territory and provide a good place to begin this work.

I will demonstrate how this approach works with an example. The dreamer had a dream that begins, "*I am living at a place like the Old Farm commune.*" He selected the phrase, "*I am living*" as his first key phrase and listed the associations as follows:

I am living—
alive, awake, accepted, a part of, active, find meaning, working, exploring, giving, serving, feeling, acting, open, loving, and connecting.

This is quite an impressive number of words. But if the dreamer wants to reach a deeper level within himself, he can take each of the words of his associations and bombard himself with questions like the ones which follow.

I suggest that you not only read these questions, but try out the technique by actually asking yourself the questions aloud. You might want to have someone else ask you the questions, or you might want to record your own voice as the questioner. For a challenging experience, brainstorm the answers in rapid sequence.

Alive—

When I say I am *alive*, what do I really mean?

Where am I *alive?*

What keeps me *alive?*

What keeps *alive* my desire to live?

What is my condition when I feel that I am really *alive?*

What is my condition when I feel not *alive* but that I should become *alive* so that not just my physical body lives?

But what is it that keeps me *alive* and makes me *alive?*

Awake—

I am *awake.*

When am I not *awake?*

Should I be *awake?*

Should I always be *awake?*

And how is the idea of my being *awake* linked to my living or being *alive?*

Can I be *alive* without being *awake?*

Would it mean that if I am *awake*, I am truly *alive?*

Accepted—

How important is it to be *accepted* by all and everyone?

Who are the exceptional people that I want to be *accepted* by?

How can I know that I am *accepted* by the Divine?

When do I really *accept?*

When do I *accept* only mentally, because it serves
my purpose?

When I am really *alive*, will I know where *acceptance* is useful, even important?

When I am *awake* and have sufficient awareness,
will I make distinctions between where I want
to be *accepted* and where it really doesn't matter?

To what extent do I go out of my way to be *accepted*?

What are the ingrained convictions that keep me
from *accepting* others?

A part of—

So *I am living*, but I am also *a part of*—the world, a
country, a city, a workplace.

And when I know I am *part of*, does that give me
the conviction that I am *accepted*, that I am truly
alive?

Can I be *part of*, and not be *awake* or aware?

And what are the obstacles to knowing that I am *a
part of*?

What is it that wants me to be *a part of*?

How important is this view?

Active—

What do I mean?

If *I am living*, does it also mean I am *active*?

What are my *activities* beyond the usual, like eating, drinking, sleeping, working?

What is my *activity* when I am *part of* something?

Am I *active* because I want to be *accepted*?

Am I *active* because it keeps me *awake*, aware,
alive?

Find meaning—
I am living, I *find meaning*.
How do I *find the meaning?*
Does this *meaning* only have *meaning* to me or also
    to others?
Is this *meaning* connected to the purpose of life?
Do I *find meaning* in *activities*, or in being *part of*
    life, or in being *accepted*, or through awareness?
Is that when I feel truly *alive?*

Working—
I am living means also I am *working*.
What's the difference between *activity* and *working*
    and being *a part of* life?
And what kind of *work* am I talking about?
Working for a living?
Working on a relationship?
Working on myself?
Is *working* necessary to *find meaning?*
Are *work* and *activity* identical or related?
When I *work*, do I become *a part of* something else?
When I am *working*, is my *acceptance* guaranteed?
And do I guarantee *acceptance* to others who are
    working?
Can I be *working* and be a sleepwalker at the same
    time?
And if that is so, then why? Or if it is not so, then
    why not?
What are the benefits of *working?*
And where are the benefits of *work* lacking?

Do I *work* for personal achievement, or do I work
to *find meaning?*
To be *accepted?*

Exploring—
To be *alive*, do I have to *explore?*
What am I *exploring?*
And what tempts me to *explore?*
What do I hope to gain or find when I *explore?*
Do I *explore* through *working?*
Or do I *find meaning* by *exploring?*
Or is it just another *activity?*
Would I like to be *part of* an *exploration?*
Do I feel more *accepted* when I *explore?*
Am I also very *awake* when I *explore?*
Is that when I know I am *alive?*

Giving—
I am living, I am *giving.*
What is it that I *give*—emotionally, mentally, eco-
nomically, intellectually?
Why do I *give* anything?
So I know I am *alive* or I am *awake?*
Or do I *give* because I want to be *accepted?*
And what do I *give* for the purpose of being *accepted?*
Is *giving a part of* a particular *activity?*
Do I *find meaning* through *giving?*
And am I *giving* to *work* with no particular thought,
or with a very definite thought?
Do I prefer to *give* of myself or to *give* money?
If I have no attachment to money, I may *give*
money.

If I have attachment to money, I may not want to
give money; I will do something else.
And what is the difference in the *giving*?
Can either one be called *giving*?

Serving—
I am living, I am *serving*.
What do I *serve*?
My wife, my husband, my children, my parents, my
friends, my employers, or employees?
Are *serving* and *giving* the same?
Am I *serving* to *explore* avenues about myself?
Can I *give* the fruits of my work, whatever they are,
for the benefit of others?
Can I *give* myself to a higher purpose in life, to *find
meaning*?
Will *serving* help me to *find meaning*?
Is *service* expressed in *activity*?
And again, when I *serve*, am I *part of* something?
If I *serve*, do I feel I am really *accepted*, *awake*, and
alive?

Feeling—
I am living, I am *feeling*.
There is a whole range of emotions that I can *feel*—
happy, angry, unconcerned, blessed, loved,
hated.
And all these emotions I will also express to others.
How much do I live through my *feelings*, rather than
through awareness, or *finding meaning*, or *working*, *exploring*, *giving*, and *serving*?

Where do I derive the greatest satisfaction from my
  feelings?

Acting—
I am living because I am *acting.*
Are *acting* and *feeling* connected?
Are *acting* and *serving* connected?
And *giving, exploring, working*—is that where I *find
  meaning?*
Is *acting* a kind of *serving* and *giving,* a kind of *ex-
  ploring?*
To be *active* and to *act:* are they the same?
What is the difference?
Acting as part of a team—a *working* team, family
  team, friends.
Acting wrongly, *acting* rightly—does it influence my
  acceptance?
And how can I become aware of the difference?

Open—
I am living because I am *open.*
Am I? I have to look at the results of my actions on
  others, and my interactions with others, and
  what I am *acting* upon—in order to find out if I
  am *open.*
Is being *open* possible in *acting* or in *feeling?*
Can I be *open* in *serving* and *giving?*
How *open* will I be in *exploring* and *working?*
In being *open,* do I *find* more *meaning* than when I
  am *active?*

Can I be *part of* a group of *open* people, or do I feel
 threatened by their *openness?*
How *open* do I *feel* in daily living?
And what would the opposite be?
Secrecy?

Loving—
Can I be *loving* and *open?*
Or do I feel embarrassed about *acting openly,* or
 having my *feelings* out in the *open?*
Do I *feel loving* and *giving?*
What would it mean to be *loving* in my *explorations?*
Can *work* also be *loving?*
Is *loving* a way to *find meaning?*
Do my *actions* arise out of *loving?*
If I am *loving,* am I more *accepted?*
Does it help me to be more aware?
When I am *loving,* am I really *alive?*

Connecting—
What does it mean to be *connected?*
Why do I need to be *connected?*
What do I gain by being *connected?*
When I am *connected,* am I more *loving?*
Am I more *open?*
Am I *acting* differently?
Letting my *feelings* be seen?
Is it *serving* that *connects* me?
And how would *giving connect* me more?
Connecting and *exploring*—where would it lead me?
To discoveries of the past, of the future, of the
 present, of the very now, of this very moment?

Does my *working connect* me?

And through *connecting*, do I *find meaning?*

Is *connecting* being *active,* or a part of a particular *activity?*

If I am *connected,* can I be sure I am *accepted?*

And will I have to be *connected* so I can be *accepted?*

Do I have to be *awake,* aware, to be *connected?*

And when I am *connected,* is that when I truly feel *alive?*

As you can see, every word in the list of associations is investigated through questions in relation to every other word in the list. The same process is followed with the next key word, *Place: location, scenario, house, scene, place of my own, place to stand,* and *a place of wonder.* Each word is investigated in connection with the other. And to "connect" things, the second list may be combined with the first. But it is best to take each by itself before going into the combination of both.

If you imagine the Divine as a huge ocean, you can find the deep in the drop through this method. When you have worked with your dreams for some time, and when you are ready to increase awareness and even the desire for awareness, then it is time to use this method. This is the next step.

You can use this same method to examine your thoughts about different aspects of the Divine. When I say *Siva,* what do I mean? When I say *Krishna,* or *Buddha,* or *Jesus,* or *the Virgin Mother, Saraswati, Radha,* or *Kali*—what do I mean and how do they relate to each other? Then you can start to understand that all these powers, to some degree, are also in yourself.

My desire has been to find ways and means of giving people the tools to do the job by themselves. But the tools have to be used and worked with, refined, and polished so the results can be discovered.

II

MIND, ILLUSION, &
WAKING DREAMS

17

Mind & Dreams

WHY DO WE have to look at the mind in order to study dreams? Ask yourself, "Where does the dream take place?" It is the activity of the mind that produces dreams. The mind can be fired by emotions, but dreams are not a function of the emotions. Mind's condition is responsible for how the dream is presented. The degree of your mind's refinement determines how you interpret your dreams. Your mental-emotional state decides what you will do and how you will do it. Therefore it is very important to consider what is going on in your mind.

Most of the time we go through our lives like sleep-walkers or like puppies whose eyes have just begun to open. We have to proceed carefully in facing our own mind, so that we do not become worried or shocked by suddenly seeing its awesome powers and not knowing how to handle them. We want to find out how the mind functions, what we can expect from the mind, and how we can increase our mental powers. In Dream Yoga we want to practice awareness of the mind at all times, even when we think we are asleep.

Finding out how the mind functions is easier through dreams than through all our conscious efforts. In our conscious efforts, mind is the instrument that investigates itself, which makes it more difficult. But in dreams we are not consciously manipulating the mind and the messages can come through more clearly. When we dream, the part of the mind that is in competition with intuition, and always wants to destroy it, is silenced; therefore dreams can guide us in furthering our own course of evolution.

Mind is the interpreter that can either allow or stand in the way of what comes from Higher Consciousness. When it stands in the way, we make miserable mistakes for which we have to pay, sometimes for twenty or thirty years—for example, if you marry the wrong person.

Mind is the creator and the interpreter. The Eastern teachings consider the mind the sixth sense because it interprets what the other five senses bring in. It interprets events, emotions, feelings. How does it interpret? It collects impressions, stores them in the memory bank, and uses them as points of reference. But do we perceive accurately in the first place? And then do we recall accurately? Our recall is usually faulty and unreliable because the senses will interfere, especially when the senses are not in balance.[1]

How are you allowing the interpreter to interpret? By what authority does the mind interpret an event or a dream in a specific way? How can you be sure that mind, the interpreter, does the work correctly? What are the influences and criteria by which the interpretation takes place?

You also have to know the cleverness and the acrobatics of the mind—how it can construct something in order to be right, how the mind can be fired by the emotional need to be somebody important, special, extraordinary. If the mind does not use discrimination, it can be very misleading. What are you feeding your emotions? What are you feeding your mind? What are you reading? What are you presenting to it? The activities of your mind in the waking state are mostly gossip, and are based on imagination. Feed your mind with material that is truly a nourishment. Do this willingly and intentionally. Do not make the Divine shake you awake. How different it is if you arrive at awareness by your own decision and desire instead of having something extracted from you.

As you learn more about your mind, you will find out how you create your irritations, difficulties, and insecurity through attachments and lack of awareness. Where do attachments come from? Desires arise from sense perceptions. When desires are fulfilled then attachment arises. Sometimes attachment also arises in

---

[1] See the dream on the importance of balancing the senses, pages 62-63.

the process of fulfilling a desire. Attachment gives rise to a mixture of passion, anger, delusion, and illusion— each creating the other. Distorted memory and loss of discrimination are the result. When you can see this self-destructive pattern, you might realize that the small *s* self must always be raised beyond its level to finally become the Higher Self.

Even if you have a certain ability to renounce, a certain degree of nonattachment, you must never lose sight of all the other attachments that remain. They, too, have to be eliminated. If they are not, you will always be a slave to your attachments. Then slavery is your destiny and there is nothing anybody else can do. If someone caters to your slavish attachments, it is like giving an alcoholic another drink. Who can ever be happy or grateful to someone who reinforces their weaknesses? Drug addicts will explain why they should have drugs, and try to convince you of their need, but yet hate you if you give them the drugs because in their innermost being they know it is wrong.

You can use reflection in combination with your dreams to see yourself clearly and to learn how subtly you manipulate yourself and others. Can you manipulate yourself into a dream? Definitely. Can you end an unpleasant dream? I think many of you have already done so. You think, "Oh my gosh, I have been dreaming!" and finally you wake yourself up thinking, "What a terrible dream!" Who is it, then, that interferes and says, "Oh, I had better wake myself up?" What is that observing aspect that can take this attitude and act on it?

There is an "observer" in us. That observer must be properly understood. The observer is not a separate entity. It is a functioning of the mind that helps us to become aware. What is it that sees? The eye sees but the mind interprets. How can we be more in that which sees? By removing the filters from what we do not want to see. In the end we blend the act of seeing, the seer, and what is seen.

The observer is different from the aspect of mind that creates images or weaves all kinds of fabrics for its own gratification and pleasure. Some of our dream stuff is created from each of these areas. In order to know where to pay attention and what to pass by, we have to know from which aspect of mind the dream material comes so that we can deal with it correctly.

In Indian philosophy Brahma is the Creator. He kept on creating endlessly until he no longer knew what he was doing. Has it ever occurred to you that there is a part of the mind that just goes on pouring out thoughts, thoughts, thoughts, regardless of what happens? In the mythology, all the other gods finally came to Brahma and said, "You can't go on like this." That is when awareness comes in and says, "What is the use of pouring out this endless stream of thought?" In moments of awareness, you can see the mind forming a sentence and at the same time speculating about a future event. The mind is tricky, and if you want to make progress you need to know it.

Meditating means stilling the mind, which is very rarely achieved. It takes a great deal of practice of watching the mind and eradicating many of the psychological problems before the mind becomes still.

Life is a constant movement, and even when awareness is dimmed in sleep, your own mind is in constant movement. Tiny stimuli, little flashes that you know nothing about, pass through the brain like trains through a railway station. The trains of thought pull out very slowly. Your mind becomes a little more quiet. And just as when walking in the dark your eyes adjust and you begin to see, so as you sleep and dream you become aware of other things that you normally do not notice. If I were to ask you the design of the floor in a certain room where you worked every day, you may not remember. You may remember only that it is somewhat light-colored. But if you were in pitch darkness where you could feel the walls only with the touch of your hands, and where the only light came from a tiny bit of moonlight or a flash from the headlights of a car, you would become sharply aware—there is a corner, and maybe over here is a door, and wasn't there a window? You become very alert; your senses become very keen.

This kind of detailed perception also goes on in sleep, while you are dreaming. If there is this much mental activity going on while one part of you is asleep, what is the difference when you are awake? Is there a difference or is there not?

We think we live in an enlightened age of great intellect and enormous technical advancement, and yet we do not know how to communicate with each other. We can invent technological wonders, yet we cannot peacefully settle our disagreements. Our lack of mental and emotional discipline has brought us to the point of having the capacity to destroy the world. Thousands of years ago the *rishis* (seers) said, "Now we see the powers of the mind declining. We shall write down the wisdom of the ages so it is not lost." The rishis were those who perceived intuitively. Their power was so great that, if you study Indian mythology, you will read of the "mind-born sons." To what extent have we lost the ability to create with the power of the mind?

Slowly we have to make our way back. Slowly we have to discover the powers of the mind. We can really understand the powers of the mind only when we understand how to manifest our dreams. If the king in medieval times wanted to read his letters for himself, he had to learn to read. It did not matter how big an army the king could call up, the scribe still had a power over him. If he wanted that power, he had to acquire it. If there are mental powers that you want, you, too, have to acquire them.

The powers of the mind are incredibly vast, but because we take them for granted, we do not even recognize them. Investigate your mind: the capacity to think, the energy used to think, the energy used to transmit thought into speech, the power of discrimination, the power of concentration. The power of memory is perhaps the greatest power and the easiest for us to understand. Where did your problems originate? From the events of your childhood? Those events are strongly and deeply imprinted in the memory.

Early childhood traumas—an accident, death of a loved one—have their effects later in life. This is quite a well-known psychological fact. But some traumas in our lives were so brief—they were simply a statement by a person in authority—that they have been forgotten. Yet the statement may have had such an impact on us that its effects can be carried throughout life unless they are traced back to their origin. One single statement— sometimes only minutes or even seconds long—why would it remain in the mind? Because its impact on the emotions was so strong.

In the Eastern theory of reincarnation, what is re- membered from previous lives are these emotionally charged events anchored in our minds and in our emo- tions. Delve into the unconscious. Discover what is there. Many artifacts that were buried in the earth thou- sands of years ago are only now being dug out. If mate- rial things can survive, so can mental things. In our dreams these memories can come up in a less dramatic way.

Dreams demand good recall. If you practice daily reflection, recollecting events, you train your memory and your observation. To strengthen your memory you have to strengthen your ability to concentrate, other- wise a great deal is twisted and intermingled with other thoughts. You can train your memory to the degree that you are willing to remember where you failed in your ideals, or where you were on the edge—it was half truth- ful and half not. This can be quite an interesting study in itself. When your memory is trained, and you have also given thought to the possibility of past lives, these memories may just roll in because the anxiety and the fear are gone. You might also think, "I'm happy to have developed enough awareness to get out of the problems I've created in this life. Now what if I am born again into another? I must be more careful."

The world can be perceived through the mind, but eventually you can arrive at another type of knowing in which consciousness no longer needs the brain or the body. This comes much later, and only to those who really incorporate an extraordinary degree of intensity into their spiritual life. First it is important to become a loving, warm, well-developed human being. It is untimely to climb to the top of the mountain unless you really have the call. And then you just do it.

EXERCISES AND REFLECTIONS

1. Mind Watch: Watch your mind for ten minutes, then take ten minutes to write down what you have observed. Continue this process for an hour each day over the next week. Read over your writing to discover the obstacles and problems that absorb your energy. You can take different colored highlighters or pencils and create a color code of your thoughts, giving each type of thought—positive, negative, forgetfulness, inferiority, anger, jealousy, and so on—a different color. See what repeats itself; then you can discover what you need to eradicate. By watching the mind, you will also learn how your mind works.

2. What characteristics does the mind have? Make a list in order of importance to you.

3. What powers does the mind have? Make a list. What powers of mind do you want to develop?

4. Review your dreams. In which dreams are you the observer? Are you observing with awareness or out of fear of taking action?

5. Write down your reflections on these questions:

How do you think?

Do you know how you think?

Do you know where your thoughts come from when you are dreaming?

Do you know where your thoughts come from when you are awake?

When does the mind become aware?

How does it become aware?

What is it that thinks?

Can you become aware of the energy that you use in thinking?

And what happens when this energy is used?

What are the results of your thoughts?

6. Pay attention to your own restlessness, and find out how the restlessness of other people affects you. When I had my first contact with Swami Sivananda many years ago, he told me to "come home to India," but not until I could sit motionlessly for five hours. I found this practice very challenging, but it led me to some incredible experiences. The restlessness in all of us is so great that this kind of effort must be made.[2] Try seeing how long you can sit perfectly still.

The need for constant reassurance also stems from restlessness. In our throw-away society there

---

[2] See Radha, *Kundalini*, and Radha, *Hatha Yoga: The Hidden Language* (Spokane, Wash.: Timeless Books, 1987), for many exercises to help conquer the restlessness of body and mind.

is always a demand for something new. Whatever the Divine does for us is not enough: "Oh, that was yesterday. What will you give me today? And what can I look forward to tomorrow?" It is up to each of us to find and recognize the finer points in our own life, and to express our gratitude for the help we have been given. If you do not have any gratitude, why should you be helped further?

18

Conscious Influences

*I*F YOU WANT to find out how your mind functions and how the conscious mind interferes with what the unconscious tries to bring up, start by watching what happens as you wake up. Is the conscious mind able to receive the messages from the unconscious clearly and pass them on? And if not, why not? What is the interaction of mental activities? What are the screens you put up that prevent the messages from coming through? What stops you from presenting these messages to yourself matter-of-factly, as they have been given?

Accurate recall of dreams is important, so when you do not remember dreams, investigate why. Is it just neglect or lack of attention? Or is it sometimes rejection of the dream's message? Sometimes as you wake up you may make an overly-quick assessment because you get worried that you might not look so good in the dream. Then you make little shifts as you write the dream down. For example, instead of writing, "I *ran* away," you might say, "I *moved* away," because it sounds better. You know that later, when you interpret it, you will have to look at what you are running away from, and you would rather not think of yourself as the type of person who runs away from anything. If you make this kind of change with your conscious mind, why should your unconscious bother to give you the message?

In other words, you want to interpret the dream in a certain way, so you prejudge the dream and therefore do not get the message. This often happens when a dream has some violent action, for example your killing somebody. But unless you find out what it is that you want to kill, you cannot judge. The individual may symbolize a characteristic that should very well be done away with. You had better kill greed, for instance, symbolized as a kind of monster gobbling food down or attacking an innocent child. But do not change the dream message ("I intended to kill him," or "I felt like I might . . .") out of the fear of what people would think. Do not make yourself dependent upon what people think. And after all, you do not have to show the dreams to anybody.

If you cannot face the dream's message, you are catering to a survival need, an artificial need that is already fulfilled. In other words, you are catering to the need of your ego. I call it a need to "survive in your own eyes." There is physical survival. There is survival in the estimation of others, such as superiors, professional peers, friends, members of the family—parents and your own children. Then there is this other type of survival—surviving within your personal concept of dignity, surviving in your own eyes. Some of our negative characteristics are too painful to admit, even to ourselves. But when we feel compelled or at least tempted to make ourselves look better at the cost of honesty, then we should ask, "In whose eyes do I need to survive?" What if it is the eyes of the ego-sense, that part which makes many of our decisions for us? What if it is in the eyes of our personality aspects which are in fierce, almost merciless, competition with other personality aspects?

Think about it. What is the use of surviving in the eyes of the ego? Is it not more important to survive in the eyes of the Divine within? Do you want to reject the message that comes to help you just because it is not pleasant? The dream may be neutral in spite of bringing a message that is uncomfortable, painful, or worrisome. In fact, it might be a blessing in disguise if properly understood. And if your attitude is correct, it may force you to pose the question, "What do I have to do?" You may think that what the dream points out is ugly, but unless the spotlight is put on it, how else would you know it exists? When you have awareness, you can make the choice to stop the ugliness. If you never see it, it will carry on for others to see.

If you want your dreams to make you look better, you have to think, "I don't want to just look better, I want to *be* better. Therefore I will listen to all of my dreams because they show me how to become better."

If you do not want to depend on other people's judgments or criticisms of you, you can instead listen to your dreams and trust your own unconscious. But then you need to have the courage to accept the "negative" dreams. You might even have to pray for that courage and ask that the dreams come in a short and clear way, so the mind cannot misinterpret the message.

Here is an example of one of my dreams that was not pleasant but was indeed a boon.

The Choice is Yours

A voice said, "You don't have to be concerned about anything except for one thing. And if you master that, you will attain union with God which is what you so intensely desire."

I asked what the one thing was.

The same voice said, "Watch, it is coming now."

I found myself vomiting out something disgusting. I tried to spit the thing out as fast as I could.

Then the voice said, "You must not say anything that is harmful to others. It is old conditioning that compels you, but you should replace this now with a deeper faith. If you listen, you do not need to fear anything. You can learn by gentleness or by pressure. The choice is yours."

The dream came in the early years, when I was experiencing so much criticism that I finally started speaking back in self-defense instead of taking things in my stride. Being shown the problem through the dream was a blessing—that has to be understood. I was clearly shown what I had to work on. The dream took me back in an instant to India and to my Guru saying, "You have to learn to accept unjust criticism and to let it go by without defending yourself and without criticizing the other person."

Dreams that deal with undesirable subjects are the most exhilarating dreams that you can have. They really tell you that you are no longer afraid to look at yourself honestly. At some time in our lives we have to decide whether we want to live with a dozen lies and illusions in heaven, which may also be one of our illusions, or whether we would rather be with the naked truth even if that meant being in hell. Once you have made the latter decision, you have no need to survive in the eyes of others or in the eyes of your own ego.

If you want to have contact with your own soul, you need to understand why the conscious mind is continually interfering with your efforts. As you become more aware and your consciousness expands, the mind will start to play childish (not child-like but indeed childish) games. It cannot bear being continuously diminished by the presence of a greater awareness. For the Higher Self, trying to communicate with the normal, waking mind is as difficult as it would be for an Einstein to explain nuclear physics to a five-year-old. It is not possible. The ignorant ego just does not know how to deal with it and becomes very silly. It is like being in a traumatic situation, when you want to laugh or do something to shake yourself out of the experience. But in the case of listening to your Higher Self, try not to shake yourself out too soon. First look at the experience that comes from the unconscious.

The ego may start playing deadly tricks. If you seriously want it out of your dreams, it may begin to manipulate your dreams and project its own agenda into your unconscious. Catching this may be difficult unless you systematically study the process and the language of your own unconscious. When you have become as aware as you can be of the whole gamut of the unconscious, you can spot the tricks. But you have to look at and understand the range of the creative aspects of the mind. That is also why practicing meditation too soon is not practical—you cannot tell when you are hallucinating, when you are daydreaming, and when you are really in contact with that creative essence within.

You may dream that you are a great priestess and wake up and tell everybody, "In my past life I was a great priestess, admired and venerated by everyone." However, if in your daily life and interaction you remain self-centered and unaffected by the dream, then the dream is obviously a manifestation of ego. If you have the dream and, instead, sincerely feel there is a spiritual significance to it, you may hesitate to talk about it. It is your secret. You will at least observe yourself and ask how you can live up to the dream's indication. If your life and attitudes change because of the dream, then you might tell someone you think will understand. But if you do not make changes in your daily life, you have not really taken the dream seriously.

If you are sincere and make a sincere mistake in your interpretation, your dreams will give you the facts in a very gentle way. They will let you know.

You may have observed in self-help groups how much admiration goes to the person who is courageous—not to the one who dodges the question, but to the one who recognizes the insight. Everybody can see that particular weakness or shortcoming, and so all admire the person who admits it, "Yes, that's me indeed!" If you experience this in a group, you must take the same attitude toward yourself.

Who in your life creates a situation you can barely accept? Who is it that pronounces judgment? It is really one or two or three personality aspects who say, "No! I can't admit that." Then you have to consider the unnecessary power that you have given to your personality aspects. It would be wise to withdraw this power as quickly as you can. Otherwise it is like putting an incapable person into a very responsible job. In a business situation you would not do this. Look at this personality aspect in the same way. Evaluate its performance, warn it of the consequences if there are no changes, and then if necessary fire it, just as you would any incompetent employee. At least put it in its proper place: "You have no business here, and certainly you cannot sit in the judgment seat."

One of my students, a sixty-three-year-old woman, said she would not talk about dreams anymore. Dream interpretation just did not work for her, and she was such a bad person that she could not even admit things to herself anymore.

I said, "I don't remember anything from our dream workshop that you have to be so adamant about."

Finally, after a whole week of persuasion, she came out with the disturbing dream. In the dream she went to the church—a very beautiful church—and met the Pope. Then she had a love affair with the Pope. She was so distressed she started crying. "Now do you see what I mean about how bad I am?"

I said, "Wait a minute. How do you think of closeness? How do you imagine oneness? What is your concept of love?"

She could understand closeness, intimacy, and love in the context of the embrace between a man and a woman.

"What does the Pope represent?"

"The Pope is a representative of the Divine on earth."

I asked her, "Were there any particular sexual feelings that came with the dream?"

"No, just a wonderful warmth and gentleness. A sense of lying really close together, not even sexual contact."

"Then what are you worrying about?"

"I woke myself up! But if I hadn't, something sinful could have happened! Then what?"

I said to her, "Even in your wildest moments your mind would never permit you to imagine yourself in an embrace with Jesus. So the next best symbol of union with the Divine was the Pope because he is at least human." I had the sense that she would soon be in an embrace with the Divine, in one way or another. "What the dream announces is that this oneness is going to take place in this lifetime—if not sooner, then at the time of your death." Then I told her several of my own dreams to help explain the symbolism more, and she was greatly relieved.

She suddenly dropped her worries and changed back into her old self again. She left the ashram with serious intentions of returning and taking up residency. But for six months I didn't hear from her. Finally I phoned her office and found that when she returned home she had had a stroke that paralyzed her from the waist up. She could not talk and had been greatly agitated because she could not get the message to me. But her hearing was not impaired, so I was able to speak with her. This is what I said, "The Pope was the symbol that showed God will hold you in his arms. You have nothing to worry about." In another couple of months she was gone.

POSITIVE USE OF THE CONSCIOUS MIND

Ask yourself, "Can I bring myself to keep all judgment suspended?" That is very important on the conscious level as well as on the dream level. If you are unforgiving of others, you will be unforgiving with similar mistakes in yourself, and at the time of death you will be your own judge. That is the Last Judgment. So learn to become more understanding, more compassionate, and learn to restrain your immediate reactions, objections, and criticisms.

The research you do on yourself is most important. Brainstorm your ideas of mind and consciousness to help overcome the power of preconceived ideas and self-imposed limitations that undercut the research. Your self-investigation has to be done with great courage, great honesty, and great sincerity. How do you do your own research and investigation? You ask questions such as, "Can I bring myself to keep all judgment suspended?" That is one question, and many more questions are bound to arise. You have to ask yourself, "How will I deal with my anxieties? What about my mental and my emotional security? How will I have to change my familiar and comfortable picture of the world?"—meaning, of course, your own personal world.

Ask yourself, "Am I willing to travel the uncharted seas of the unconscious?" That is exactly what we do when we research ourselves—we chart those seas. We want to discover what is there. We want to know where the undercurrents are, where the rifts and cliffs are beneath the surface, and this is risky business.

Then ask, "How will I deal with my anxieties? If I anticipate that some phenomena—prophetic dreams for instance—have a basis in reality, how will that alter my mental perceptions and interfere with my mental and emotional security?"

A psychiatrist I met in one of the big cities said, "You know, I had an extraordinary and clear dream of your ashram after you were here the last time. Is there a guest lodge, a small office and bookstore, and an old house where you eat meals?" I said, "Yes, exactly."

He went on to describe details of the grounds and then asked, "And is there a young man there with particularly large blue eyes?" He gave other details of the man's appearance.

"Yes. Why don't you come and see for yourself?"

He eventually did come, and as I walked around the ashram with him, he pointed out landmarks he recognized from his experience. A young fellow with particularly large blue eyes walked by and he said, "That's him, the one I saw in my dream."

Then the psychiatrist became frightened. He had to accept his dream experience because he had verified

it through his visit, but he did not want to accept it. Fear! "I have to change my perception of the world." Fear! "I have to change my perception of my life." Fear! "I have to change my idea of what my senses can do." Fear! "I have to take more responsibility for what I perceive." And, of course, a lot of pride was at stake. He had signed up to stay at the ashram for ten days but left after several hours and stayed at a motel down the road. It was too much for him.

So you have to ask yourself, "How will I have to change my familiar and comfortable picture of the world?" In that comfortable picture of the world, there are no phenomena because there is no empirical evidence of any. Yet there is an enormous amount of evidence outside our own social, educational, and racial setting which we have just never put together.

Technological men will say, "Yes, we can build rockets. We can go to the moon, and we will soon go to Mars and Saturn." If we can build complicated devices that lift us through the barriers of the gravitational field, then what, symbolically, can take us beyond the orbit of our own minds, beyond our mental gravitational field? If the mind can create equipment on the physical level that can overcome the much greater forces in outer space, is it not logical to think it can also overcome strong barriers to expanding awareness? What the mind can create, it can also do. Scientists are quite clear about the barriers surrounding the earth: gravity, the electromagnetic fields, the Van Allen belts, and so on. What are the barriers of the mind that prevent awareness from expanding? Awareness needs to use all that extra power that the mind usually expends on its own barriers. What are the forces similar to gravity that push possibilities down and pull you back to the densest atmosphere? Fear, survival, desires, and mental background noises are the ballast that prevent you from taking off. They keep the messages of the unconscious from coming through.

The Higher Self is trying to initiate a clarification process, but if you are full of yourself or set in your views of what is possible, it is very difficult. The more you empty your mind of its residue, the more insights you can receive. This process will lead to greater awareness, which is the characteristic of consciousness. Only then will a wide range of mental powers surface.

EXERCISES AND REFLECTIONS

1. Observe yourself carefully to catch the tendency to change a dream as you write it down. Observe where you feel that it is too painful to look at the truth. Ask yourself, "Would I rather hold onto the illusion of a better opinion about myself than face the facts?" Keep in mind that at some time you will have to face the facts, and if you refuse to listen to your dreams, the facts will be given in a much less gentle way. Working with your dreams gives you the opportunity to cooperate with your own evolution.

2. Write down your dream exactly as it is before you even begin to assess it, and make a carbon copy. Later you can divide your dreams into what you consider positive and negative dreams. When you see that you have enough positive material, perhaps you will not need to try to fool yourself for survival's sake.

3. What would "surviving in your own eyes" mean in your life? What do you need to survive emotionally?

4. Write down a dream that is very exciting and thought-provoking, one that you think you will remember quite well because you had a strong reaction to it. Sign your name to the dream, date it, then put it into an envelope and seal it. Recall the dream a month later, writing down exactly what you remember. Open the envelope and find out what changes (or distortions) your memory has made.

5. If you want to know intensely enough why certain circumstances recur again and again in your life, there is a method that will eventually lead to understanding. On Monday evening briefly write down your experiences during the day. Put the paper in an envelope, seal it, and put the date on the envelope. Do the same on Tuesday, Wednesday, Thursday, Friday, and Saturday. On Sunday write down what you remember of your entire week, without referring to the envelopes. Then open the envelopes and find out what you missed, what you twisted, what you changed. You can extend the time to two weeks, and again write down all you remember from those two weeks. Stretch this to two months, three months, a year. And if you record your dreams during the same time, you will be amazed to see how sharpening your memory changes your dreams.

This method requires tremendous effort. But if you do it, you will learn more about your life, and about the mistakes you have made, and what has led to the circumstances of this life. You will see where you could have made different decisions. If you make the effort, you will eventually be able to recall any event in your life. After two years, you will be able to recall events of past lives.

6. Ask yourself these questions:

   How reliable is my memory?

   How reliable is my perception?

   How do my senses interfere and twist the facts?

   What or who makes the changes in my memory of events?

7. Ask yourself:

   Can I bring myself to keep all judgment suspended?

   Am I willing to travel the uncharted seas of the unconscious?

   How will I deal with my anxieties?

   How will I deal with my mental and emotional security?

   How will I have to change my familiar and comfortable picture of the world?

   What are the barriers of mind that prevent awareness from expanding?

19

The Unconscious in Daily Life

W E HAVE SEEN in investigating dreams how the unconscious can present its messages through dreams, and we have just looked at how the conscious mind can influence these messages. But does the unconscious also influence our waking lives?

Is there anyone who really lives by reason and logic alone? In the Western world these qualities are claimed to be the highest attributes of mind, but is that true? What logic and reason can create is one thing, but we also need to discover the irrational mind and its capacity to create something quite different. In the same way that we look to dreams for messages, we can also look at symbols in waking life. What catches our attention? Our eyes are directed by the unconscious.

When you first open your eyes in the morning, what do you see? The clock? Is time an important element in your life? Have you ever thought about what time is? Find out. If you have flowers in your room, and you are attracted to the bright red ones, does that indicate that you need a little stimulation in this day? If you are attracted to flowers of a beautiful amethyst color, perhaps you need a day in which you are more subdued, like this softer color. If your attention is drawn to a healthy green plant, does it represent your health? Your growth? Or do you find the plant too plain and look for colors?

When you get up and go to your clothes closet, what you choose reflects something of your mood. What should you wear today? A white shirt, a pale yellow one, a bright pattern, long sleeves, short sleeves? Something festive? Something simple? Something subdued? If you wear a belt, what kind of belt? Do you need to tighten up? Do you want to decorate yourself? Are you constantly belting yourself with self-reproach?

What your eyes fall on in your house often has something to do with your state of mind. You may focus on all the doors and windows, and then suddenly a door opens and hits you, and you begin to ask yourself why. Maybe there is a door you should not go through. So your sense of observation becomes refined and you pick up the cues from your own actions. Eventually you do not depend on your dreams alone.

If you notice that your gaze keeps going back to the telephone, perhaps you should stop and ask, "Is there someone I should contact?" It may not mean that you should phone that person, but perhaps you should write or communicate in some other way. If we gradually allow our intuitive capacity to open, we will begin to use more than the one-fifth of our brain that scientists say we now use. What about the other four-fifths? Would it not be interesting to have access to even the next fifth instead of just functioning with a fraction of our mental capacity?

If something pleasant attracts your eyes, then it probably reflects the state of mind in which you happen to be. If you keep noticing the unpleasant or undesirable, this is probably the outcome of what is going on in your unconscious. As you observe yourself, your hidden desires will also come to the foreground of awareness. You will start to understand yourself in a deeper way.

A woman once commented quite emphatically to me, "Why do people buy these artificial flowers? I think it's terrible—now even flowers are artificial! What else will become artificial in our lives?"

One day when I visited her home, she had a beautiful flower arrangement. But when I came closer to admire it, I saw that it was an arrangement of artificial flowers. "Why did you change your mind?" I asked.

"I don't really know. It's hypocritical isn't it, after what I told you and everyone else. I just don't know why I bought them."

I said, "Well, let's sit down and have a cup of tea. Maybe we can find out."

It was obvious to me. She was going through a difficult phase in her life—a divorce—where she felt no joy, no color. She could not afford to buy fresh flowers every few weeks, so to bring some brightness, color, and joy into her life, she had bought these artificial flowers. She could keep them as long as she wanted to and get rid of them when she wanted to, and they would not die like the marriage had died. This showed me that when we need to bring balance into our lives, we may establish this balance by very peculiar means, even against our own very strong convictions.

Symbolism is essential because we cannot take the whole truth at once if we are struggling for survival and acceptance. That would be too difficult. However, if we do not get to know ourselves, we will always blame others for our own mistakes, oversights, and negligence, because the ego cannot take criticism. At the same time, the soul cries, really cries. Sometimes we do not know why we cry. But if we constantly put our inner self down and hurt it, one day by our actions we may extinguish the inner Light, and it will be by our own doing.

My father had a friend who was one of the well-known psychiatrists in Germany, and as a child I was sometimes sent to his office to invite him to dinner. Often I had to wait a long time. Once when I was sitting in the waiting room, there was a patient waiting there, too. I had brought lots of paper and pencils with me and the man asked if he could borrow some. I gave him what he wanted and he started doodling. When the nurse came and called him into the office, he looked at the paper, looked at me, and then decided to leave his drawing behind. I kept the paper. Later, at the dinner table, I asked the psychiatrist, "What did this man tell you?"

He said, "Oh, that's not for you to know. But why do you ask?"

I replied, "I think he's going to shoot himself."

"Why would you think that?"

I showed him the doodle. He could not see the gun in it until I pointed it out to him.

As a psychiatrist he was more tuned in to *listening* to what his patients were saying. After this incident he shifted his attention to *seeing* the messages of the unconscious. He experimented by putting out paper and pencils and asking me to come and spend an hour in the waiting room. Sometimes he would come to the house and ask, "Well, Sylvia, what do you make out of this picture?"[1]

The unconscious gives us clues about ourselves and others. We have to find out what it tells us. The clues come from the unconscious because the conscious mind is always so busy—always occupied, sidetracked, diverted—that it rarely ever listens. Think about it and find out the extent to which you live by symbol and metaphor. You will be amazed that your daily life, which you thought was lived so consciously, is really so controlled by the unconscious.

~

We have to get to know our inner selves, and we can sometimes check out our inner characteristics by looking on the outside. If you are always trying to look different from others, it implies you are comparing

---

[1] Much later in my life I developed workshops such as "LifeSeal" and "Music and Consciousness," which use this same principle. Participants draw material generated by the unconscious, and in the process of interpreting their own symbolism, discover the many worlds within themselves.

yourself and are in competition. You can impress people with your clothes, jewelry, and watches, but only temporarily. As soon as you reveal yourself a little more—perhaps in the second meeting, perhaps in another five minutes—the advertising image fades and people ask themselves, "What's behind it? How much reality is behind it?" Those who project a false image fool themselves only for a little while. Eventually it leaves an accumulation, a residue of wrong actions and attitudes that interferes with what they really want to do and to be.

If you want others to see you as a helpful person, become truly helpful. If you want to be seen as a good friend, find out what it means to be a friend. Then you will be seen for what you really are. You become real. You will not have to worry about people seeing through the image you are presenting, or what will happen when the show is over. A show lasts only so long, and when it ends, the effect is quickly forgotten. If I look back at how many premieres and big shows I have seen, I cannot recall even one immediately. But I can recall a schoolteacher who was extremely warm and helpful.

I asked many men who had been prisoners-of-war what sustained them. Many said it was an image of a good person in their lives—an old schoolteacher, a professor at the university, or a clerk in the corner store. It was not someone who had created a fireworks image, a flash that quickly goes out—"Ah, wonderful!"and then it's gone. Those images we do not remember, so what is the point of constructing more? We all want something lasting, so we have to sit down and reflect on what is lasting in ourselves and go after that. Then we can live in peace and harmony and with less anxiety.

If we allow ourselves to be more influenced by our own symbolic messages and to pay more attention to them, we will become more creative, and our lives will become much richer and so much clearer. If, for example, a woman begins to notice that she is not standing up straight, she can begin to discover what is behind her bent posture by asking herself questions, such as, "Am I not taking a stand? Can I not stand up for myself? Am I feeling bent over by the weight of some burden? What is it?" This process of self-discovery is much more acceptable to her than if another person comes along and says, "Look. You are like this and this, and these are the changes you must make." She would probably feel insulted or harshly treated.

Investigate very carefully. Paying attention to image, symbol, and metaphor in daily life gives you the freedom to learn from yourself rather than from the criticism and judgment of others. The more attention you pay, the more guidance you will receive from your inner guide. Then you will discover that you have not only an inner teacher or Guru within, but also a really good friend who is very happy and willing to take care of you, if you let it happen.

There are lovely pictures of Jesus knocking on a door that has no handle on the outside. The image conveys the message: the door has to be opened from the inside.

~

Clarify what you mean by two words: "symbol" and "image." Do you use the two words interchangeably?

For instance, if you see a beautiful image of a Buddha, is the image different from the Buddha as a symbol? When is the Buddha a symbol? Is the Buddha a symbol only of a religion, or could it be a symbol of something else? If you see people prostrating before the image, you might think, "What strange behavior. Why do they do this?" Because to you, the Buddha is only an object, a piece of carved wood or stone. But to the trained Buddhist, the image of the Buddha is a symbol of the state beyond mind.

In the Christian teachings we talk about Jesus as the Son of Man, the Messiah, the Good Shepherd, the Son of God, the Lamb of God, the healer, teacher, and carpenter. Though we speak in different ways of Jesus, it is always the same person. But how do we create in our minds an image of Jesus not as a person but as the symbol for Higher Consciousness or Christ Consciousness? To create that image we have to clarify the words we use to symbolize Higher Consciousness—which really has no image—otherwise we only create confusion in our minds.

In the same way the chakras in the Kundalini system are not just images.[2] They symbolically express the exercises that need to be done to understand the full potential of each level of consciousness, which leads to becoming fully aware.

If we look at a picture of Radha and Krishna, are we seeing an image or a symbol? It is both. Krishna is in a human body because human beings can only understand the Divine, the Cosmic Energy, in terms of their

---

[2] Radha, *Kundalini*, chakra plates.

own image. But to show that he is not an ordinary human being, he is given the color blue, which implies the vastness of the sky. As human beings we want something greater than ourselves, so we picture the Divine in this way. The other aspect is Radha, who symbolizes Creation. Creation is symbolized by the female aspect in Hinduism and Buddhism because in pregnancy and giving birth, a woman's capability is very obvious, while paternity is not obvious. Radha represents the Creative Force manifesting, and all that has been brought into being. Radha loving Krishna and Krishna loving Radha symbolize the Cosmic Forces loving Creation, Creation loving the Cosmic Forces.

In the same way, you can look at what images and symbols you have woven into your own life and what effect they have on you now. What do your father and mother mean symbolically? We forget what we have put into our own young minds. Very often the problems we have later in our careers and personal lives are linked to the residue of those old images. If your father was too busy to play with you, and your mother said to him, "You have to punish little David," you may know the father only as the punisher, the one who forbids and lays down the law.

When you are a grown man or grown woman, you cannot let these old images cling to you. They are leeches that rob you of your energy. You have to look at the residue of all these images and symbols that are still lingering in your mind. If you can reach the point of understanding that, while your parents may not always have made the best choice, they did the best they could with what they knew at the time—then you free them and also yourself.

When you came through the door of your mother's womb to enter life, you had no clue about the kind of world you were entering. When you enter spiritual life, you cannot know what this life will be like either. One North American Indian tribe symbolized this entry into the unknown through a ritual called the "Ring of Fire." The actual ring of fire on the ground symbolized knowledge. You have to have the courage to walk through the fire to the safety of the center from which knowledge emanates. It takes courage to enter because wherever you enter, you do not know what you will meet.

EXERCISES AND REFLECTIONS

1. Try to define your terms "symbol" and "image" by using examples from your own life. Start with your family. What symbol was your father to you? What image do you still have of him? Was your father the ruler of the house? Was he the judge? The punisher? Was he the provider? The care-giver? Was he the financier? Was he the builder of your life within the setting of the family? Was he the destroyer? (Perhaps you remember once long ago building up your blocks and he laughingly knocked them over, destroying a creation which was very important to you.)

2. Then look at your mother. When you were small, she was probably your comforter, your nourisher. But did she also admonish you, even as a little one? Was she your teacher but also your disciplinarian? Did she create but also destroy hopes? Perhaps she

was a source of pleasure. Perhaps she seemed enormous, like a goddess. For little children the father and mother are like a god and goddess of immeasurable power.

3. After thinking of the images and symbols of your family, look at your own human body. Stand in front of a mirror—sometimes with different clothes on, sometimes with no clothes. What kind of image do you present? Do you like the image of your body? Is your body a symbol? And if your body is a symbol, what is it a symbol of? Indulgence? Harshness? Health and healthy living? The body is like a book that can be read.

4. Look at your face in the mirror. What does it say? Kindness or resentment? Is it a face that can express hope, concern, trust?

5. Another way to find out about your thinking is to listen to what you say. The unconscious speaks, but we have to listen.

6. Can you expand your creative ability and enrich your life by incorporating symbol and metaphor more consciously into your life? As you go about your daily work, you can bring in symbolic meaning. As you wash the dishes think, "May my mind become as transparent and sparkling as this glass." When you are ironing or making your bed, ask that your mind become free of its wrinkles.[3] When you wash your car, think of purifying your mind.

---

[3] Swami Sivananda Radha, *Symbolism in Daily Life,* audio cassette, (Spokane, Wash.: Timeless Books).

When you clean up the clutter in your back yard, think of clearing away the clutter of old concepts in the back of your mind. By doing this work, you do not have to expose yourself to other people's criticism.

7. It is hard for people to listen in a waking state. Most people hardly listen to their own thoughts, much less to anybody else's. Have you ever wondered why all the gods and goddesses have beautiful earrings? The ear that listens is precious. How else could you show that an ear is precious? You can make a fist and hit somebody, and with that same hand you can gently hold somebody. So the goddess may wear a bracelet of lotuses to symbolize that the hand that can heal is precious.

Today jewelry is worn as body ornamentation. It no longer symbolizes preciousness. But you can use your jewelry consciously as symbolic reminders: earrings for the precious ear that hears; rings or bracelets to symbolize the hand that can touch with love and reach out with compassion; necklaces to express your desire to turn self-will into divine will.

20

Waking Dreams

NIGHT DREAMS AND daydreams are made of the same stuff. They take their powers from the mind. We have to look into our thought processes of which we are usually unaware, otherwise they can run away with us and we become the creator of the good and the bad in our lives. In order to know ourselves, we have to look at the many images that pass through the mind, especially images triggered by emotions. Investigate them very carefully, scrutinize them, and find out what effects they have.

What is the difference between daydreaming and dreaming during sleep? We have many dream tendencies in the waking state. If we let the mind interfere, it will twist perception in different directions. Each of us tries to put an image across to the other, but we do not know whether or not we succeed because the images are interpreted by another mind. And each mind writes its own scripts with its own dream qualities: beautiful woman, ugly woman, good man, bad man, threatening person—yet none of these may be accurate. We have to make the effort to look at the facts as they are.

Years ago a president from one of the top universities came to see me and was very upset. A couple who looked like lower-middle-class people had met with him and were asking many questions about the university. He had treated them brusquely. He later found out that these insignificant, lowly-looking people were ready to donate two million dollars to his university, but they changed their minds and gave it to another university. He was very angry. I asked, "Does everyone with an I.Q. of 150 wear horn-rimmed glasses?" We create these kinds of stereotypes—how a wealthy person looks, an intellectual, a doctor, and so on.

In the spiritual field there is just no end. Twenty people will have twenty different images of a spiritual leader. I decided early in my life as a sanyasin that if I wanted to play those kind of games, I might just as well have stayed in the theater as a dancer. Why would I give up a comfortable life to keep playing the same game?

Some people may project a threatening image onto another person. Why would anyone want to make another more threatening? Because it increases their self-importance. It is as if they are saying, "Look at how I am able to deal with such a formidable individual!" They create distortions.

Sometimes, too, you may think you are being intuitive when you are really acting from past conditioning. For example, you may be suspicious of somebody, but that suspicion may arise from the law of thought association—their red hair and green eyes remind you of someone else who disappointed you or treated you violently, so you unconsciously fear that this person will do the same. You cannot afford to carry on this kind of oversimplification. You have to study the law of thought association as it applies in your own life.

As you observe yourself, you will see how difficult it is to understand new experiences by themselves. They are always seen in the light of old experiences. Just looking at the color blue or red, looking at a bald head, looking at short hair or long hair or blond hair or red hair, looking at somebody with glasses—we continually associate. And if we have formed very strong opinions, we judge others in an unthinking way. We may tell ourselves, "People who wear glasses can't see what is right in front of them," and then we function on the basis of that assumption.

Most of us are perceiving inaccurately. It is extremely difficult to perceive clearly. You may do so in a few areas, but in some areas you will simply have a blind spot and find it hard to shine the light onto that spot. What is even more difficult is not knowing that the blind spots are there.

Here is an example. Let us say there is an Oriental carpet hanging on a wall. We are seeing it from a distance, too far away to be able to say exactly what it is. I might think that it is very interesting wall paper with a medallion in the middle. You might disagree and think it is a carpet with a medallion in the center, which is hung on the wall. I defend my perception that the design is wallpaper, stating adamantly that carpets belong only on the floor. We might argue back and forth without getting anywhere. If somebody else comes along and says it is wallpaper, you might start to wonder whether your perception is correct. If three people say it, you might even come around to agreeing that it is, indeed, wallpaper.

This is brainwashing. Someone says there is only one way to understand what you perceive, and because you gain acceptance by seeing it in the way you are told to, you start to see it that way. This can happen throughout your life until finally you do not accept your own perceptions anymore. You just run with the crowd—this is what you are told to believe, so you believe. When you *believe*, you have no need to investigate or to question. But when you really want to *know*, you will make the effort to investigate and find out.

Advertising takes enormous advantage of ignorance and tells you that something is good for you or is even better than the competition's product, and therefore you want it. We can call this hypnosis. If you are sufficiently hypnotized, you will eat certain things that may not be good for you, put certain cream on your skin that you do not really need, and so on.

Our whole way of life is quite conditioned. If somebody says the opposite of what you believe, you will find it difficult to accept. You may cry and feel upset. You have been conditioned to accept something as truth without really knowing, without having checked it out. In fact all our problems arise ultimately out of previous conditioning. The mind is like a computer which is programmed in a certain way, and when you are requested to act against the program, the mind does not know how to handle it.

Let us take an example from religion. Suppose that you have been told and believe that only through Jesus can you be saved and go to heaven. Then when you study at university you find that scholars are debating whether there is any historical evidence of Jesus' life. Your belief system, which had been programmed into your mental computer, will be upset. You may feel your whole life is thrown off balance because you had lived with this particular belief. Now what can you do?

Perhaps you will intellectualize your way out of the dilemma, or perhaps you will give up on Jesus and accept another belief, which you do not know any better. If somebody says you should not really believe in that, either, because there is no historical evidence, you may throw up your arms in despair and ask yourself, "Where does this leave me?" It leaves you with the option of suspending belief and suspending judgment. You can step out of your belief systems instead of letting them automatically drive your mind. You can say, "It sounds interesting and possible, but I have to find out if this is really so." Whether there is a historical Jesus or not, however, you can tune in to the Christ Consciousness that Jesus represents. You can do this by repeating the Lord's Prayer five hundred times a day, or by learning the Sermon on the Mount by heart and repeating it to yourself. Through experience you will attain a different kind of knowledge.

Your unconscious will give you guidance where your logical, conscious mind cannot. You may have to believe certain things for a certain length of time, but only until you know for yourself. You know only when you experience.

~

Investigate your process of thinking. Find out how the mind creates its own picture from partial facts. If you look at something, let us say a microphone, and you do not really know how it functions except that it catches sound and transmits it somewhere else, your imagination may take your incomplete knowledge and become quite creative. You might say, "There is a very complicated connection of wires that receive the sound; vibration travels along them and then is decoded . . . ." You may present your guesswork with so much conviction that it sounds *as if* you know. We do that very often. When we do not have all the information, we add speculations as if they were facts. But that information has no level of reality. It is simply manufactured by our minds from very tiny fragments of facts.

If I see a person I do not know, and I am not clear about the workings of my own mind, I will put together a number of conclusions, consciously or unconsciously. Most of the time we do this unconsciously. I might say to myself, "Well, this young man wears glasses, dark pants, and a white shirt. He is very clean-cut so he must be decent and hard-working. He must work in an office, and he is probably quite intelligent." Then I think I know what this fellow is like and how he behaves. I draw all

kinds of conclusions, but by what means? Mainly by the creativity of my mind, which is fed only fragments of fact.

If somebody else comes and tells me her perceptions and opinions of this man, my mind weaves this in. My whole picture of him is the outcome of the creativity of my mind. If I then meet him, he may think, "She really doesn't know me. I must let her get to know me better." But this will be impossible if in my mind I have already decided what kind of person he is. The image I have created of him then becomes his rival, and I may never know what he is really like.

Life is very complex. If we understand this, we can be more forgiving and loving with each other because we know that such misunderstanding can happen anytime to anybody. The mind is forever weaving fabrics with any little bit of thread and material it can get. Is there any truth in those weavings? No. If I do not allow you to really make yourself known, the image that I have of you cannot be true. It is an illusion that I create and harbor.

Sometimes we have an illusory idea about God. Once you have formulated an idea about what that energy you call "God" is, you have a concept in the same way that you have a concept about another person. That concept becomes God's rival in your mind. That concept is your illusion.

$\sim$

Fantasy, daydreaming, and hallucination are all powers of the mind. What is referred to, really, is the skillful or unskillful use of imagination.

Daydreams are strings of images that do not have any particular intention or aim. The fire of emotions is not behind them, nor is the fire of the desire to truly create. I can daydream that I am the most beautiful woman in the world, or the most intelligent. If we dream and then do not do anything about our daydreams, the mind is set adrift and we lose a lot of energy.

When we daydream we create a fantasy world to live in, and we create a fantasy image of ourselves. We create one fantasy after another, especially about other people, until something unpleasant happens, and we wake up and say, "Oh, I didn't expect this. I didn't know you were like this." We do this because we lack the courage to see what is.

Perhaps you created a fantasy of togetherness. You made yourself believe in a love that did not really exist. You did not care to investigate whether or not it really existed because you were happy with the fantasy. But then, the marriage breaks up and you have a rude awakening. The facts present themselves. After twenty or thirty years of marriage you may have created a world of your own. When your partner walks out, this world collapses because suddenly you realize that the fantasy of togetherness never had any reality; otherwise, it would not have collapsed.

In the practice of yoga we lay the foundation by slowly, slowly seeing what is. "I see. The act of seeing. And what is seen."[1] That which is seen, has it any reality? Or do you see only the fantasies of your own mental creations? Occasionally you may be able to give life

---

[1] Radha, *Kundalini*, 133.

to a fantasy and then you think, "Ah, it's real." But for how long? When you create a fantasy, the fantasy exists only on your own powers. The moment you stop empowering it, the fantasy collapses.

What do we feed our minds? It is very important to know. What fantasies do we indulge in? Many people in psychiatric wards create their own fantasies and then believe in the reality of that world. Hallucinations are just a stronger type of fantasy, in which the power of imagination and emotions are undisciplined and succeed in overcoming reason.

When my Guru was anticipating the problems I would encounter in the West on my return, he said, "I see dark clouds gathering in the West." My mind could create the most powerful, dramatic, destructive dream out of his words. If you sit long enough with something like this, you can actually create the situation, or at least contribute to its creation. If we involve ourselves in a negative daydream such as depression, at that moment sickness can slip in. And sometimes our own powerful mind also prevents us from getting better or from creating a more positive script. If our dignity, reputation, or sense of self-worth were torn down by destructive criticism and we accepted it, we can become that weak, worthless individual and see ourselves that way.

~

We each have our waking dreams. We may fantasize our dream house or we may dream of discovering the cure for cancer. The motivation for our dreams can vary, from personal fame and gain to great compassion. Sometimes it is a mixture, like a cocktail, with a little of everything in it. But because it begins as a dream in the mind, we do not anticipate the various stages of the process which are required to make the dream come true. That would disturb the perfection of the dream. When our waking dreams do not come true, we feel pain. From a yogic point of view, this pain is self-created.

I have often been invited to sit in on workshops led by psychologists who wanted to talk to me about them afterwards. In one such workshop, a woman broke down and cried, and people clustered around, patted her shoulder, and said, "Don't cry. We all love you. You don't need to cry."

When the psychologist saw that I was very uneasy with this, he said, "You obviously want to say something?"

I said, "Yes. This is the biggest lie. Under the circumstances your gestures could not be more dishonest. This woman is really suffering, and now everybody assures her of their love. But if she takes her two small children and comes to your house and says, 'Can I stay here until I find a job?' what happens to your love? Right now you selfishly want to make yourselves feel good, but there is not one tiny grain of truth in it. Fantasies." That is what it is. We create a make-believe world for ourselves, and we create a make-believe world for others and tell them to live in it, that it is real.

Then, too, we believe so strongly in the reality of our own existence that we do not want to look at death. But if we do, we may find it is not so different from moving from one room to another. At death, we move from one dimension to another. Really, there is no need to fear.

～

How powerful the mind is to be able to create and dream things up! Its power is enormous. Every woman and man carries an image of a dream lover.[2] This is a different kind of dream, but we have to recognize its existence, too. For the woman the dream lover is always tall and good-looking. He is always doing the right thing at the right time. He is a great protector, very romantic, and a great lover, of course. He has sufficient money or perhaps is very wealthy. So when she meets a man she checks off his qualities against her dream lover list. Men do the same. Who can measure up? The dream lover image is never examined realistically. Could there be such a person?

The dream does not change the wife or the husband, nor does the dream bring the dream lover into the picture just because it exists in our minds. When the image does not tally with the reality of the human partner, there is trouble. Because we cannot manifest the dream lover directly, we can create the opposite and make ourselves into someone who does not deserve the dream lover—we are too guilty, too bad, too ignorant, too ugly—which creates feelings of insecurity and worthlessness. Many women after they get married try to maneuver their husband into being the man that they really want. But he is not the dream lover, so there is a constant edge, a constant battle.

There is no ideal relationship. Even the one created in our minds is not ideal. That is why we are disappointed and feel lonely, even if we are married. That is

---

[2] See Radha, *From the Mating Dance to the Cosmic Dance,* for more discussion on the dream lover.

why we feel hurt and left out and try to get over this feeling of loneliness. We are born alone and we die alone—what do we really share? We can share something material, but what goes on inside is completely individual. Each mind interprets in its own way. The ideal relationship is a daydream that many people try to turn into a reality. You expect something that cannot exist. What will you do? Either force the issue to try to make your dream come true, or resign yourself to the fact that your dream picture changes simply because other dreamers dream different dreams. Two people may temporarily dream the same dream because they have the same desires, but once their desires are satisfied their lives go in different directions again.

In movie and television advertising we see the young couple who are in love joyfully running through a field, hand in hand. At this point in their love affair they are focused only on the sun, on that one beautiful day in paradise. But we cannot stay in paradise. When you are forty or fifty years old you have to rethink your images. Why? Because you have matured. You have learned not just to see the sky of your imagination, but also the horizon. You see the light and the shadow and learn to accept both.

Some people have romantic fantasies about past lives. One woman thought she had been Queen Mumtaz, for whom the Taj Mahal was built, not even realizing that it was a tomb, not a castle. She was an ordinary housewife who wanted to be somebody. If you want to be somebody, then do something about it. Learn, study, practice, acquire a skill. Become unique. But fantasy or daydreaming will not contribute anything. In fact people will dismiss you as someone caught in illusions.

Great difficulties arise from daydreams because the power of illusion is enormous. Some people do not recognize their illusions for what they are because the desire to be recognized and accepted, and the need for a greater sense of self-worth, stand in their way. Discrimination is absolutely essential. Once you have gone through enough pain and disappointment, you start to see how you have lived through illusion and with illusion to such an extent that you are constantly disappointed and constantly hurt, especially in your pride.

If you realize how much of your energy is taken up by your illusions, desires, and emotions, and if you can instead shift that power to the attainment of Higher Consciousness, you have discovered a real bargain. Most people do not even know that such a bargain exists. It is through pain and disappointment that you finally come to see what you are doing to yourself. But should it take a thousand lifetimes, a hundred thousand lifetimes, a million lifetimes? The price is too high. Do it now.

EXERCISES AND REFLECTIONS

1. To work with daydreaming or dreaming in the waking state, write these "dreams" down and take the key words out, just as you do with nighttime dreams.

2. You can also take a situation in daily life—especially an emotionally charged one—and look at it as if it were a dream.

What is the setting?

Who are the characters?

What is the action?

What is your position as the *I* in the dream?

Which *I* is it?

What is the resolution, or the question you are left with?

3. Look at all the expectations that you have, even in conversations with other people, as dreaming in the waking state.

4. Examine your sense perceptions.

   Do you know which of your senses are dominant and which less developed?

   Are any of your senses in competition? For example, if a person appears pleasant to your eyes but sounds terrible to your ears, you may reject him or her because your sense of hearing overrules sight. You may even think that you are making a wise judgment based on logic and reason, or intuitive perception. Find out how this applies in your life.

   When you make snap decisions, how much are your sense perceptions responsible?

   How reliable are they?

   Try listening to a person while you are doing some handiwork. You will really hear what the individual says. If you look up at the person, you hear only half of what they are saying because the face very often conveys a different message from the voice.

When these two messages are conflicting, communication is off-key.

6. Review your dreams and find out which senses are active in your dreams. If you can bring all five senses into your dreams and recall their involvement, you will sharpen your sense perceptions in waking life. This will have a big impact on your life because we experience life through our senses.

7. Cultivate the senses by paying attention to how they operate. Spend a week investigating one sense. You may become aware that you have just scratched the surface.[3]

8. Try answering these questions:

What is the power of perception?

Is the power of perception on the mental level?

Is the power of perception intuitive?

Is the power of perception sensual?

Is the power of perception the same or different if it is intellectual or intuitive? Is it separate?

How can you assess the power of your perception?

How can you become aware if your power of perception expands?

Does it mean you have greater understanding?

Is the understanding more a knowing of the heart or a knowing of the mind?

---

[3] See Radha, *Kundalini*, for more instructions on how to investigate the senses.

9. Find out where your past experiences interfere with clear perception.

   How do you unconsciously apply the laws of thought association in your daily life?

   In how many different areas does it come up?

   Do you use this power beneficially?

   Does it always undermine your own security?

10. Ask yourself:

   What is a dream?

   Who is the dreamer?

21

Directing the Power

INSTEAD OF BEING caught in illusion, you can use the same power of imagination to create something worthwhile. One way to do this is through creative visualization. If you feel very unhappy, yet you are not at the point of being able to deal with your problems directly, I can say, "Sit down, relax, close your eyes, and let me take you into a world of fantasy. Let us go into a beautiful garden where you can hear the gentle sounds of a brook, and see an array of flowers and birds." When your imagination becomes involved, you can continue to explore and complete this picture. In this way you can change a negative, destruc-

tive mood into a positive one.[1] The problem that created the despair will not necessarily go away, but you can at least temporarily release pressure from the nervous system and the emotions. Then in the same way that I led you into the fantasy, I can perhaps point out that what you despair over is only a different fantasy, a different dream.

To develop a positive use of imagination, the mind has to be given direction. If I want to invent something, I have to put my desires and imagination into focus and give them a boost from my emotions. Then I can be creative and bring my dream into fruition. If a daydream is just the fantasy of the ego wanting to be somebody special, nothing much will happen. Creativity requires the use of will—taking action. The difference between the artist and the daydreamer is that something will emerge from the daydream of the artist, while the person who is egocentric and thinks of himself as a hero, or thinks of herself as the most beautiful woman in the world, achieves nothing beneficial. It remains an illusion that is bound to get shattered.

We have to recognize that one of the driving forces behind our night-dreams, daydreams, and illusions, is desire. We scheme to fulfill those desires and spend most of our lives in the attempt. From this thought process or dreaming we begin to act. Some people act quickly, and for those with powerful emotions, the actions are compulsive. But if you are sincere, the Divine will also create the circumstances to fulfill your good desires if they benefit other people as well. My Guru said, "Dream

---

[1] See also Swami Sivananda Radha, *The Body-Garden* and *Guided Meditation,* audio cassettes (Spokane, Wash.: Timeless Books).

that you are a saint and you will become one." But then you have to put your dream into action; you have to think like a saint. He said to me, "Think of yourself always as Radha, and nothing is impossible." The Bible says the same—if we have faith, we can move mountains, we can do what seems impossible.

Desire creates, or is the instigator that creates, the images in the mind. When we visualize the image strongly and clearly, we work to bring it into manifestation. If you want to manifest your dreams, go through the creative process in your own mind. You need both your dream and the desire to manifest it. Then you can bring your chosen path to fulfillment. Sometimes you have to cut back a bit on the grandness of your dream to make it possible. If your expectations are too high, they are often of the ego. You already know that you will never achieve them because they are beyond the human capacity to achieve, so you have created a beautiful excuse. If your wishful thinking is wonderful—great. Keep it. But you must not deceive yourself into believing that the wish is already a reality in your life. The dream may be showing you what you can become but you may not be there yet.

If your goal is to be a success in business, and if you put in the effort, which might include more education or specialization, you can fulfill your potential in your career and make it a success. But if your dream is to become a self-realized person, extraordinary efforts have to be made. If all your attention, time, and effort go toward daily living, then what can you expect to know about spiritual life? There will come a time when you must decide what you want to do with the rest of your life, because whatever you acquire materially cannot be taken with you. What do we take with us?

All religions speak about life after death. What do you mean when you think of a soul entering heaven or the Oriental idea of rebirth? Unless you make changes now, in this life, how could you be any different after you die? What more would you know simply because you are free of the cage of your body? Try to imagine a vortex of energy—consciousness—which encapsulates all that you are mentally, emotionally, and spiritually, and which includes the energy that controls the body, and memory itself. Science agrees that energy is indestructible. You can change energy, but you cannot totally destroy it or make it nonexistent. The vortex of energy could then assume another place to live, another time to express itself, cultivate itself, perfect itself. This is what could be reborn.

We can say, "But aren't philosophy and spiritual life a dream, too?" Yes, but they are a dream from which we can benefit, a dream that nourishes us differently, a dream that brings a greater state of awareness, and a dream that gives rise to quite a different mental power. When we clarify our ideals by asking, "What kind of person do I want to be?" that is also a dream, but it is within the realm of possibility. I can dream that it would be wonderful to be healthy, to have a positive attitude, and not only smile, but let that smile come from my heart. If the dream is entirely related to myself, then it is within my capacity to manifest it. But I have to recognize its importance and develop the powers to bring it about.

Some things we cannot bring about with the limited powers of mind we have today. I will not say they are impossible, but we do not have the necessary ability to keep the mind single-pointed over extended periods of time. We have to build up certain powers of the mind first, and then our dreams can become a reality. We have lost contact with the true knowledge of who we are. We have forgotten our divine origin, our inheritance, and have become trapped in the encasement of human existence.

To help us understand our potential we can look at mythology, which is really the symbolic history of humanity. Consider the myth of the young gods from mid-heaven who descended to earth, pulled by their own curiosity.[2] When they resided on the earth for too long, enjoying themselves, their beautiful ethereal bodies began to harden. The ethereal body or vortex of energy, when too long exposed to the earth's atmosphere, adjusted to it and finally lost its ability to return.

We are the young gods from mid-heaven. Or, if you take the story from the Bible, we are the fallen angels. If we take the very early Egyptian Gnostics' view, we are the soul descended into matter that enjoys the union so much that we do not want to return to our heavenly home. But God, who does not want to abandon the soul, makes sure that we eventually remember our origin, and long for our real home.

Think about it. How are you using your God-given intelligence? You can make the choice to become aware and to start the journey home.

---

[2] See excerpt from *Ekottara-Agama XXXIV, Takakusu II, 737,* quoted in Radha, *Kundalini,* 339-340.

If we direct our minds by focusing and concentrating on an image, we can discover the mind's powers. Leave the smorgasbord of images behind, choose a single one, and pursue it. See what happens. Choose an image that can change your life. That is precisely what you do with the Divine Light Invocation. You create in your mind an image of Divine Light, and fill your body with this Light. Light is a symbol for the divine energy and has been used by many religions for many centuries. By practicing the Divine Light Invocation, you reinforce your desire to become a being of Light who will bring Light and joy into the lives of other people and greater joy and fulfillment into your own life. By continuously focusing on the Light and by inviting Light into your life, you will become a different person.

Here are the instructions for practicing the Divine Light Invocation, which is one of the most important practices for establishing and maintaining contact with the Light within.[3] With the Divine Light Invocation, you permeate all you are with Light. There is nothing greater than the Light, which is the most subtle symbol for the Divine. By permeating your whole body with Light, you automatically drive your ego out. Focus on this. You want to let the light of understanding, the light of love, grow. Your own growth and development will take place much more easily in the light of wisdom rather than in the artificial light of theoretical knowledge.

---

[3] Please refer to Swami Sivananda Radha, *The Divine Light Invocation,* (Spokane, Wash.: Timeless Books, 1990), for a complete presentation of the Invocation: the history, preliminary concentration and visualization exercises, and benefits of the practice.

THE DIVINE LIGHT INVOCATION

Stand erect, feet shoulder-width apart. Inhale. Lift the arms above the head at the same time as you smoothly and gradually tense the whole body. The arms should be kept straight and the tension maintained throughout the body. Hold the tension and the breath. Keep the eyes closed and focus them on the space between the eyebrows. Make the following affirmation to yourself, with all the concentration possible:

I AM CREATED BY DIVINE LIGHT
I AM SUSTAINED BY DIVINE LIGHT
I AM PROTECTED BY DIVINE LIGHT
I AM SURROUNDED BY DIVINE LIGHT
I AM EVER GROWING INTO DIVINE LIGHT

Use the imagination to *see* yourself standing in a shower of brilliant white Light. See the Light pouring down upon you, into the body through the top of the head, filling your entire being. Exhale as you slowly lower the arms. Now, without raising the arms, keeping them at your sides, tense the body and inhale. Hold the tension and the breath. Mentally repeat the Invocation. Slowly exhale and relax.

During the second repetition, with the arms beside the body, concentrate on *feeling* a warm glow of Light suffuse your entire body, outside as well as inside. Acknowledge silently to yourself:

Every cell of this, my physical body, is filled with Divine Light; every level of consciousness is illumined by Divine Light. The Divine Light penetrates every single cell of

my being, every level of consciousness. I have become a
channel of pure Light. I am One with the Light.

The Divine Light Invocation is an exercise of will,
as well as an act of surrender. Be receptive to the Light
and accept that you are now a channel of Divine Light.
Express your gratitude with deep feeling. Have the desire to share this gift with someone you wish to help.
Turn your palms forward.

You can now share the Divine Light with any friend
or relative. See him or her standing before you. Mentally open the doors of your heart center and let the
Light stream forth toward the feet of this person. The
Light encircles the body, spiraling upwards in a clock-
wise direction, enveloping the body completely. See the
spiral moving high up into the sky, taking the person's
image along with it. Finally the person merges into the
source of the Light and becomes one with the Light.
You may even lift your head to follow the spiral of Light,
keeping the eyes closed. When the person has passed
from your view, relax and silently give thanks for having the opportunity to help someone in need. Remember, in helping others we are helping ourselves.

If your concentration weakens while you are practicing the Divine Light Invocation, repeat the exercises.

Learn to put people into a spiral of Light, and keep
yourself in the Light so that only the Divine in you is
actively in the foreground.

The Divine Light Invocation may be used as a Mantra or positive affirmation, as well.[4] Repeat the words of
the Invocation to yourself and see yourself surrounded

---

[4] See Radha, *Mantras,* for further instructions on Mantra practice.

by Divine Light in your daily life. It will help you to keep in touch with the Light within you and to see the Light in others around you.

EXERCISES AND REFLECTIONS

1. Use the Divine Light Invocation many times during the day. If you are having difficulty with another person, put that individual into the Light. It will diminish any hostility you may feel and any hostile individual will also slowly change (perhaps not to the satisfaction of your emotions, but everything will take place in due time). Do not let your practice become routine or it will no longer have an effect and will become a mechanical process that has no meaning. You have to involve the emotions, and you may find that the emotions are very helpful if they are used correctly.

2. Think about Divine Light. Reflect on each line of the Mantra.

3. Try to contact the body of Light through your practice of the Divine Light Invocation. As long as you are alive, there is a tiny speck of energy—you can call it Light, you can call it life force—in every cell of your body. Recognizing your own energy and becoming aware of energy in every cell of your body is important. This concentrated focus takes time to develop. Start by cultivating the imagination, because creative imagination opens the door to a different kind of perception. Perceiving your own body as a mass of Light is an extraordinary experience that you will never, ever forget.

4. Another practice for gaining awareness of the Light is learning to see the Light around everything.[5] Take a grain of rice between two fingers and hold it up against the sky. Maintain your focus on the grain of rice until you see a halo of Light around it, a tiny force of Light emanating from it. When, over time, you have achieved the ability to see the grain of rice emanating Light, place the grain in a silver bowl and present the rice as an offering to the Divine. It can be part of the treasure chest of your efforts to move toward the Divine.

5. See if you can observe the shine of life in each petal of a freshly-cut flower. Then watch it over the next few hours and the next few days. Can you see the shine from the petals slowly disappear, even though the color may not change? The energy, the inner Light, is gone. The same thing can happen with human beings—the body may die later, after the Light of the spirit is already gone.

6. When you feel miserable or depressed, you can turn the image of Divine Light into a more personal divine image. It is just as if you are creating a balloon with your imagination and painting on it a picture of Jesus, Buddha, Divine Mother, Siva (whichever is your favorite), knowing that the energy which fills the balloon is divine. The image satisfies the emotional need for personal contact with the Divine. The Light will be there when you are able to receive it, but the image will be there, created out of the Light, when you need the image. It is like seeing the Light in different frequencies, different

---

[5] Radha, *In the Company of the Wise*, 36.

pulses, and different colors. One day the Light and the image may oscillate, so that you see first the image, then the Light, the image, the Light. Light is the only image that is so fine, so ethereal, that any image you visualize can be dissolved into Light. Finally, images will dissolve into Light by themselves.

7. The whole process of working with dreams will bring about an evolution toward the Light, because the mind's production of the dream is nothing but a play of Light in different colors. Dreams give you the way to see yourself through their prism. If you put your activities into the Light, your dreams will also become quite different.

8. Even if you have an experience that is just a flight of fancy, you can still work with it and see if you can get to the bottom of it. Although it may be just your wishful thinking, your desires and imagination can prepare you for experiences of a more serious nature. If you want Light in your life, think about Light, invoke the Light with your imagination. That is the preparation. One day you will have it. You will know true experiences because they will turn your life around—you just cannot remain the same person.

9. The degree of your intensity in the practices relates to their effectiveness. You can support your direction by intensely concentrating, even for brief moments throughout the day, on a spiritual thought, a Mantra, an image, or a prayer, or by feeling an intense desire to be with the Divine.

22

Dream? Illusion? Reality?

Y OU CAN EXPAND your investigation of dreams in the waking state. Do not think of just one particular type of daydream, but ask yourself, "How is my whole life like a dream?" Where do I make up my own nightmares and get involved in them? Suddenly you may catch yourself and wake up, realizing that you are creating a mental reality that you do not need to stay involved in. Find out if there is another reality to which you can go— though not as an escape. You can never "escape" to a greater reality.

Sometimes you will see that this greater reality can be transmitted to you through a dream, and sometimes you will recognize that daily activity is like a good or a bad dream—that certain realities are not as solid as you think.

Think for a moment about how creative the mind is. We can produce an enormous amount through the power of the mind, if we really look at it. We can have an awareness that certain things exist only in our mind, nourished by our emotions. One example is psychosomatic illness, the product of imagination. Another is a woman who believes she is pregnant and has all the signs, even the placenta and the milk, but no baby. How did she produce these signs? She cannot tell you. But she had an almost fanatical desire to have a baby. All the power of her emotions went into that single-pointed idea in her mind, creating the process in her body. So the emotional power of desire can create a situation that is at least a partial fulfillment of the desire. Would you say the ability to create the changes in her body was real, or just an illusion, or a "partial" reality?

Some yogis do fantastic experiments and practices, for example locking themselves for years in a single room without the influence of light, just to find out how creative the mind is. Yet at the same time, they take their dreams very seriously. Why would such people pay attention to dreams? Precisely because dreams can be the thorn that removes the thorn. By seeing how creative dreams are, they may come to contemplate reality and find out how each day is like another dream.

The experience of dreaming can be a model that helps us understand the unreality or illusions we create in our own lives. In dreams we suffer only temporarily, until we wake up. You may dream that you hurt yourself and experience the pain with great intensity. You may dream you are separated from someone you love and feel the emotional pain, until someone wakes you up. When you wake up to the greater reality of Cosmic Consciousness, you will see life and its suffering as a dream. But you have to experience this directly, not just entertain an intellectual concept about it.

Looking at life from the philosophical standpoint of *Maya* (that the world is illusion), you may ask, "If this waking life isn't real, why bother with the life of the unconscious?"

As long as you are walking around in a physical body that can feel aches and pains, you have to realize that this physical level of reality has some power. If a person has to have a leg amputated, you cannot say, "Your leg is just an illusion. You never had that leg in the first place." I know my body exists and has come into being by some means. If I say it is through the power of the mind, I have to reflect on what that means. If my leg were to be amputated, where is the power of mind that can create another leg? And if I have created the whole body, why can I not do this?

Mixing an intellectual understanding that "life is illusion" with the fact of our existence can create a great deal of confusion and uncertainty in daily life, making things very complicated. This confusion often happens when people read Eastern texts intellectually, without having really absorbed the teachings as they should be absorbed. We have to be careful and discriminating, and ask, "What is the reality of this physical life? What is the reality of the mind? What do I really know?" If you have only read about this idea without acquiring the knowledge from practices, you might imagine yourself among the elite of thinkers. But do you really know, or have you just accepted and believed without thinking in depth?

"Knowing" means knowing from experience. To attain true knowledge you need extraordinary power. The mind requires the tremendous force of a rocket that can penetrate the gravitational field of the earth and then is free in space. Once you go into the "outer space of the mind," you may indeed gain quite a different understanding. Only from that liberated perspective can you look at life and see it as illusion. While still living in the enclosed atmosphere of desires and the gross sensory perceptions, you cannot fool yourself and say, "I have heard about Liberation and I've read about it, so I know what it is." The mind is not capable of penetrating its barriers that easily.

What can you gain from brainstorming "reality" and "illusion" that you can apply in your daily life? At least discover where you create your own illusions. You have to be willing to face the untruths, the false beliefs, and the tainted ideas that you have about yourself. Start with practical steps and take one step at a time. Lay a good foundation. Otherwise any earth-shaking discovery can bring all your mental constructs crashing down. Once you know something from experience, you will never feel hurt if others disagree with your view. The foundation you have built becomes so strong that it cannot be shaken by any opposing concept.

From your exploration of daily life, you can then begin to investigate other levels of reality. What is the relationship between space, time, and the unconscious?

What are the different levels of consciousness? Right now if you were to try to contemplate seven levels of consciousness, you could not. You know to a limited extent, and not even accurately, three levels because you live in the three-dimensional world. If you have some spiritual experiences, you have put your foot slightly into a new dimension, the fourth dimension. But even if you have had a great number of spiritual experiences, you still cannot anticipate what the fifth dimension would be like, or the sixth, or beyond. You have to lay the foundation before you can explore even the possibility of a fourth, fifth, or sixth dimension.

At one point you may question your understanding of time. From a certain perspective you might understand that reincarnation has meaning only as long as you accept time as you now know it. When you go beyond the general understanding of time and space, even reincarnation disappears. The one hundred thousand lifetimes that you may have had to this point are simply perceived as one life; what you consider your current life is like a day between nights. Just as you do not cut your life into little bits and pieces and think you are a different person at each stage of life, so all lifetimes in a sequence of one hundred thousand may really only be one.

~

So ask yourself, "What is reality?" A word for "reality" exists in all languages. If the word exists, there must be something that *is* real. The human mind cannot think of anything that is nonexistent. We are usually aware of the physical, tangible world, the world that we experience through the body, and which includes the universe with all its galaxies. That is one reality. But what about the reality of the energy that pervades it all?

In yogic thinking we live in three worlds—the physical world, the mental world, and the spiritual world. That means we can also have illusions on the physical level, on the mental level, and on the spiritual level. We have to be sure that our spiritual experiences are true experiences, not imaginary movies. But although we can have illusions about the Higher Self and the spiritual world, that does not mean that the spiritual reality itself is an illusion. The physicist may not be able to see the particles, but the traces are recognizable. If the traces are there, then something must exist that created the traces.

How can we recognize the traces of the cosmic reality? Every day you breathe. Can you separate your breath from the air around you? Your breath becomes visible only under certain conditions, in certain temperatures. Those outward conditions are not the result of your own power. In the same way, every now and then Cosmic Energy will let you know of its presence by creating a condition where you can see that power within yourself.

Here is another example. You might stand overlooking the lake and say, "How beautiful this lake is!" But what do you mean by "lake?" Lake is water, and water is a combination of two gases. Yet you do not see two gases constantly intermingling. In the same way a certain reality is not necessarily so tangible to your senses that you can see it in its original state. We have to overcome the limitations of our senses on the gross level.

As you sit, you know your body, you know your size, you know your weight, you know your reflection in the mirror. But that which came into existence and made the decision to manifest, what does that look like? You cannot even know what your own self-created thoughts look like unless you give them an image. An invention may start from very abstract calculations, but if it is to manifest, there has to be a picture in someone's mind, nourished by the desire to create and by the power of imagination.

How does the power of imagination connect illusion and reality? Where does illusion end and reality begin?

The dream of flying probably arose from a desire for freedom, a desire to move without restraint. The image of flying preceded the creation of the machine that could manifest the desire. If you had dreamed about an airplane before airplanes existed, that dream would have been your illusion. But if you took your dream and invented an airplane, that manifestation would have a tangible reality. Once whatever you dream about comes into manifestation, it has a certain reality. Once the airplane existed, further ideas arose rapidly, developing the thing itself, making it more and more complex, faster, bigger, until years later we developed jets, and now we have rockets that can take us to the moon and beyond. Once we have created something, events take their own course. But everything that is now manifest started at some time as an intangible idea.

So the relationship between illusion and reality has to be very carefully contemplated. If we had not had a desire to fly, the airplane would never have been created. The moment you pick up an idea by the sensitivity to the creative power, this idea takes hold of you and in turn, breeds a desire to manifest. Then you get busy scheming how you can manifest your desire. And if your desire is single-pointed, you will get it. It will manifest—in due time and in proportion to the degree of your intensity. Then when it is created and it exists, you cannot say that it is an illusion. The illusory force, having been very subtle at first, has now condensed. The idea has condensed into the manifestation of whatever we desire.

Let us assume that we once existed without this body, that consciousness existed as energy. You were consciousness per se, and had all the perceptions associated with your senses. But now we come to an impasse because it is impossible to imagine energy-as-such. Even nuclear physicists, who have exceptionally well-trained minds for abstract thinking, cannot think of something intangible, unimaginable. So we have to create an image for that pure energy in order to be able to deal with it. Then you have to remind yourself that you have done so, in order not to confuse the symbol with the energy itself, which cannot be explained by words.

We can imagine consciousness as a vortex of energy like a tornado. Although we cannot see the air current itself, we can see its funnel shape from the dust which the tornado has picked up. Similarly, consciousness holds the dust and seeds of memory and past actions. And now we can come to another understanding of human existence here on earth. Life has always existed here, but perhaps the human mind needed a properly prepared vehicle for receiving the energy of consciousness. The brain is that vehicle, and the body is the vehicle for the brain. Once the body has manifested, we cannot deny its reality.

At some time we have to recognize that our body is not what we usually think it is, but is a vehicle to be used for the attainment of pure consciousness. The body, in other words, has to be recognized as a spiritual tool with which to attain to the ultimate. Then we do not deny the physical reality, but recognize a greater one.

As you expand your thinking, you will see that your mental reality is transformed. This transformation is a process—new concepts are born and others will "reincarnate" within ourselves. Eventually we will move toward the state of liberation from all limitations that are a weight, that are restrictive, and that keep us in our self-fabricated prisons.

What is dreaming up this life? Get in touch with that and you will be in touch with the reality of your innermost self.

~

There is a saying in the Puranas[1] that Vishnu dreams the world into existence. Life is the Divine Play, although sometimes the dream looks random.

We can see that each of us creates our own world by dreaming different types of dreams. As we become more aware, we can start to ask, "Why should I dream about problems and difficulties when I am the creator of my dream and have the power to change it?"

We can even dream about all the beauties of spiritual life, but we might find that our own materials—

---

[1] The Puranas are legendary histories of ancient India, and are the principal scriptures of Vaishnavism and Saivism.

the threads from which we weave the dream—are not always strong, or clean, or long enough. We might make mistakes in knotting, or tie some threads too tightly. So our dream cannot be as perfectly realized as it is in our minds or desires.

We have to learn how to weave the thread of our dreams into the design of the Divine Play and not get tangled in the attachments of the world.

EXERCISES AND REFLECTIONS

1. Learn to watch all the images flashing by in the mind without identifying with any of them, because if you identify with them, you become involved with them. You do not want to become unnecessarily involved with the contents of the mind. Write down those thoughts and images that come again and again, and finally look at each one squarely, straight on: Is it so important? Is it my ego? Do I need to assert myself? What happens if I don't? Am I stepped on? Or am I just experiencing karma coming back to me?

2. It is best to practice reflection before attempting to practice meditation. When you can recognize what is going on and throw out the creations of your mind, and finally put a stop to them, then you are beginning to make progress. The problem in the West is that most people have not done the preparations before they try to meditate. If you do not try to sit motionlessly for three to five hours and face the wrestling of your mind, you just do not know what the mind can do.

3. Put certain pictures and objects in your room— a picture of the Buddha, Jesus, Divine Mother, Krishna—whatever image of the Divine most appeals to you. Whenever your eyes glance at them, immediately, by the law of thought association, you are reminded that you have been dreaming, daydreaming, that you have clouded the awareness of your true nature, of your true state of awareness, of your Higher Self.

4. Often in the West we assume that reality is something concrete. If you think, for example, that the table is solid, I suggest that you sit and stare at it for ten minutes and then record what you see. Even science tells us that what *appears* to be, may not be what is. Can you look at a large lake and see it as a combination of two gases?

5. Observe yourself. That which you look at, do you see it? What is the act of seeing? And what is it that you see? Is there indeed a moment where the three—the seer, the act of seeing, and what is seen— blend into one?

6. Ask yourself:

   What are my concepts of dream, illusion, and reality?

   Is there more than one level of reality?

   Where does illusion end and reality begin?

   What is the reality of a dream experience?

   What is the reality of daily life experience?

   If I knew that everything was illusion, would that remove the dramatic, painful obstacles in daily life?

III

DREAM YOGA:
JOURNEY TO THE LIGHT

23

Dream Yoga Practices

REAM YOGA requires first the willingness to train the mind even to remember dreams, and then the discipline to carry through specific practices. You have to become aware of the personal language of your own unconscious, which is based on the impressions from many lifetimes and on the influences of your present life. You also have to deal with what emerges from the unconscious in your daily life, and discover how you create your own illusions and realities. After you have established a good foundation by understanding your own symbolism, and after you have explored mind, illusion, and reality as presented in the earlier parts of this book, you may be ready for more specific Dream Yoga practices.

Some of these practices may seem a bit disconcerting because you have to break with well-established habits, not only of thinking but even of living and sleeping, if Dream Yoga is to be truly successful. For example, you may think you need eight hours of sleep every night, but that is not necessarily so. Because in the same way that you nourish your body by what you eat, you nourish your mind and heart by what you think and do. Spiritual practices nourish the feelings of the heart and release the pressure of emotions.[1] By nourishing the heart, a higher part of the mind will eventually open. Then, if you really want the Divine, you will experience quite an extensive influence of the Divine through your dreams.

The most important quality in the practice of Dream Yoga is your sincerity. Insights will arise from the sincerity of your hope, willingness, and receptivity. Your constant focus on the Divine will bring you closer—both when you are awake and when you are asleep. Whatever you do in your waking life—driving your car, washing dishes, or typing on the computer—you have to cultivate the awareness that you are always in the presence of the Divine. If I want to know who you are, I have to become involved with you. I have to be able to observe your responses to me. If I do not get any response I will try harder until I do. It is the same in becoming involved with the Divine. I have to try until I get a response. When I elicit even a faint response, I have something to build hope on. If I stay involved, which

---

[1] Spiritual practices include prayer, Mantra, Divine Light Invocation, and reflection. Refer also to Radha, *Mantras* and Radha, *The Divine Light Invocation,* for more specific instructions.

means to be in the service of the Most High, it is likely that I will receive a stronger response.

Staying involved with the Divine means developing the ability to visualize at will—a feeling, a thought, a divine image, Light. This requires concentration, the ability to maintain single-pointed focus. To practice Dream Yoga, you need to control the mind, which is extremely difficult and requires the same intensity of concentration that a surgeon needs in performing a new type of surgery. You have to be right there—not somewhere else at the same time. When I was first learning to develop single-pointedness, I would sit with a big box of matches in my lap, and attempt to say the first line of a four-line Mantra, keeping out any other intruding thoughts. Any time a thought came in, I would drop a match onto the floor. When the match box was empty, I realized how difficult it is for the mind to stay with one single line of thought. I often suggest that people work with their favorite prayer in the same way. When you do achieve that concentrated focus, you come to a resting place where the body-mind no longer interferes. The body-mind is simply pushed aside, and you may have an extraordinary dream or experience.

Eventually, through daily practice of reflection leading to meditation, the power you gain will carry you through day and night, sleep and dream. When you have imbued your mind intensely with a desire for the Most High, this desire itself will become a guiding light. As you learn to keep your focus directed, you increase the chance of contacting or recognizing the Light in sleep.

Working with Dream Yoga will bring you to the point where you can discover that the spiritual world is not an illusion. The mind is capable of such incredible dreams that you will be challenged to ask, "What is real? And how do I move from this world to that?" You become aware that everything is relative. Is your dream the reality?

~

Instructions for Dream Yoga are part of Eastern yoga practices,[2] but these are not easily understood by a modern Westerner since the teachings were part of a different culture. Certain cultural laws become anchored in the human mind. Those laws become a forceful, controlling reality in our lives. Only under a great threat (or more rarely, a great passion) will we be persuaded to go beyond them.

Often, too, terminology is used in the Eastern texts that is not explained because it was written for students immersed in the philosophy. Another cause for misunderstanding is that the Eastern mind functions differently from the Western—the Westerner takes everything literally, whereas the Eastern teacher expects you to understand through intuitive perception. For example, one of the Dream Yoga instructions is to investigate carefully what causes rapid awakening from dreams; if there is too much tension, you should relax more. You are not told *how* to relax, but obviously what is meant is not just lying down and relaxing your muscles. You relax by looking at that which makes you tense.

---

[2] Dream Yoga is one of the six yogas of Naropa. See Gharma C. C. Chang, *Six Yogas of Naropa & Teachings on Mahamudra* (Ithaca, N.Y.: Snow Lion Publications, 1963), 88-94. Also, Herbert Guenther, *The Life and Teachings of Naropa* (London: Oxford, 1963), 67-69, 183-188. See also W. Y. Evans-Wentz, *Milarepa*, for an example of Dream Yoga in action.

However, I think that the essential meaning, technique, and aim of Dream Yoga teachings are quite understandable to us and can be put into practice now, to our great benefit. When I recognized that what I loosely termed my "sleep" was really a different state of mind, and "dream" was often a meditative experience, I asked myself how I could help other people attain this same state. The following practices are ones that I have used and can recommend to anyone wishing to get in touch with that greater reality.

First train yourself to observe the mind and to retain the memory of your thoughts while falling asleep. Watch the images that flit by and explode into emotions. Observe your breath. Breath is the best indicator of balanced or unbalanced emotions—emotions that can be as harsh as anger and violence, or as sweet as attachment and other illusions. Observe the many colors of emotions, as well as the shades from black to white. Try to *watch* yourself fall asleep.

Practice holding your rosary or your mala, or a special ring or stone, throughout the night. Use any object with meaning from your tradition and culture. You might choose a sacred object or a stone from your favorite pebble beach. Or you can write a prayer or a very important intuitive thought on a small strip of paper and roll this paper into a tiny roll. Then try to keep the object in your hand without letting it go; if you do let it go, train yourself to wake up immediately. This indicates that your awareness is focused where you intended it to be.

Then you can begin the practice of visualization. Create an image in your mind of the Divine Source. For most people it will be easier to concentrate on a concrete form than an abstract idea, just as it is easier to visualize a beautiful flower and to imagine its fragrance than it is to think of the flower as a combination of chemicals. Light is the most subtle image grasped by the mind. The same spiral of white Light that you visualize going up in the Divine Light Invocation, you should now see surrounding your body or your entire bed like a cocoon as you sleep. Then throughout the night try to maintain that connection with the Light—"holding the Light" as you sleep.

Holding the Light during sleep is one of the key instructions for Dream Yoga. How can you do this? By becoming very familiar with the Divine Light Invocation and by exercising your ability to visualize the Light. Being able to maintain contact with the Light during sleep requires rigorous practice on a daily basis. Eventually, through this regular practice, the power will become more steady.

Bring in the Mantra as your last thought in the period immediately before falling asleep. Your Mantra might be the Divine Light Mantra, or *Hari Om,* or *Om Namah Sivaya,* or the Divine Mother Prayer.[3] If you need help in removing your mental-emotional obstacles, call on Siva. If you feel you have lost your way, call on Krishna to play the flute and call you home. You can also use any sacred words that symbolize the Most High to you—calling on the name of the Virgin Mother or Jesus, or repeating "Jesus loves me" from the Christian tradition, or repeating a line from a prayer in whatever religious tradition you come from. See if you can main-

---

[3] See Radha, *Mantras,* for discussions of these Mantras.

tain this involvement with your Mantra or your prayer throughout the night.

When I first started watching dreams I made a pact: "I will remember my dreams only when there is something important for me to know and to learn, but otherwise I will stay with the Mantra." When, through constant practice, you can keep the Mantra going until you reach the point where you wake up in the morning with the Mantra, then you are over a big hurdle, because during the six or more hours that you sleep, the most important part of your mind is with the Mantra. Then you do not need to worry if you have time for meditation in the day because you have accumulated the mantric power in yourself so intensely that you do not even lose it in sleep. But this is only one plateau. Do not rest there, although you can at least be assured that all the sacrifices you have made to reach this point were worth it.

The gradual development of the ability to remain focused on the divine word and image depends on how much work you do on yourself. It is almost a superhuman effort if you have not first removed the psychological obstacles. All practices have to be done with awareness. If you find that you are going off into a trance, minimize your practice. All powers that come to us, even divine powers, should be under control. No power that we cannot control is good for us, even if it comes directly from the Divine. But in conjunction with the practice of awareness, there will be no trance.

Some practitioners of Dream Yoga sleep in a certain position to try to remain aware while the body sleeps. The sleep position recommended for Dream Yoga is to lie on your left side (with one leg drawn up to relax the abdomen), close your right nostril with the back of your left hand, and breathe throughout the night through your left nostril in order to have only the spiritual current active for regenerating the physical body and the various levels of mind. This position also influences the contents of your dreams.

See what happens and find out what kind of dream you have in the morning. It is quite possible you will turn over ten minutes after falling asleep. But you can gradually train yourself to sleep at least a few hours on your left side, breathing only through your left nostril. Eventually you may be able to hold the position for four or five hours. Be truly observant and make careful notes.

This alone—maintaining a certain alertness and letting just the body sleep—is a very difficult achievement and will take quite some time. However, if you have ever been deprived of sleep, for instance as many people are during wars, you may have learned that this is possible. I remember being on the subway in Europe during the Second World War, and while my body was standing asleep, something in my mind would be aware and say, "Six stations from now you must get out." I knew precisely where I was, what I was doing, and where I was going. These peculiar states of mind appear extraordinary only because we have not paid enough attention or tried to find out how the mind works.

I remember when my Guru was going to explain the position to me, he said, "First show me how you sleep." We were out on the open patio which had a cement floor, but that didn't matter. I lay down on the cement to show him. "Aah! And why do you sleep this way?"

"I always sleep this way. I don't know why." My natural sleep position was, in fact, the exact position prescribed for Dream Yoga. Past lives? This is possible but it is also possible to pick up what is needed from other minds, because the interaction of minds becomes quite expansive. The busier we are, the less this happens, of course.

One of the Eastern Dream Yoga practices is to focus on the throat center and to worship the Guru in the throat center.[4] The Guru in the throat chakra is something that can only be understood if you have worked with the Kundalini system. Then you will know that the throat center is the center of surrender. To follow instructions, you have to surrender. To listen to someone, especially the Guru within, you have to surrender the merry-go-round of mental conversation in your own head, otherwise, you will not hear what is said. The word "Guru" does not always refer to a physical human being. The Guru, in this case, is the essence, the energy, and the capacity to surrender. That which is surrendered—self-will—has used energy to express itself, frequently as stubbornness, throughout life. When the expression of self-will is removed and surrender is achieved, then by the sincerity of your undertaking that energy becomes a guiding Guru in future actions.

Some schools of thought encourage people to manipulate the contents of their dreams in order to create a situation that they want. But do you not already know

---

[4] Chang, *Six Yogas,* 89.

what you want? Why would you need to manipulate your dreams? To what end? If you already have illusions about yourself and do not even realize it, and then you try to manipulate your dreams, you will never know who you really are. All the personality aspects will just fight among themselves. Many people are able to manipulate dreams that are at a psychological level. But if you want to step out of the psychological and have contact with the Divine, you have to maintain your focus on the Divine and *surrender* to the wisdom within. Then your dreams will change in a way that is quite dramatic.

When you can maintain the Light in sleep, wrapping yourself in Light, and filling yourself with Light, you will stay in a receptive frame of mind, open to divine influences. When the self-generating power of the Divine Light Mantra is achieved and can be extended into sleep, if dreams do come, they often take on a very different character. They become direct messages. You can contact your divine essence and learn that there are as yet undiscovered places of Light from which great wisdom emanates.

Your continuous work with Dream Yoga will make it possible for you to approach a certain part of the mind more intensely. When you have passed through certain "gates," as I call them—the first being the psychological, then the instructive—you will eventually come in contact with a hidden place of the mind, a higher mind that most people rarely even know they have. What you discover is not something given by an external power. You have just cleared the garbage away and let emerge what has always been there.

Then you will have very different dreams—dreams that seem more real than life itself, dreams that will in fact give a perspective of more than one life. Through this kind of dream, you open a secret door—a door to the Eternal Light. Then you begin to realize that you are not who you think you are. You may have climbed Jacob's Ladder far enough to say, "There are no further rungs to climb. I can now be lifted up by the power of the Light."

But an exclusive focus on the Light is necessary if you want dreams to lead you to the Light, and to a recognition of the Light within. If you are only theoretical, you will never achieve anything. To experience the hidden meaning of dreams, you need to have an intense commitment to the pursuit of awareness. As long as there is greed—not necessarily for material gain but for recognition, to be seen and heard—certain types of dreams will not occur because the degree of surrender, absolute receptivity, and the strength of intuition are lost.

While we now live in the physical body, which is a "dream body" that cannot go with us at death, we will eventually live in a body of Light. This has to occur. Sleeping focused on the Light is a preparation for death, which will make it possible to be reborn into a higher state of understanding and eventually into the enlightened state.

SUMMARY OF DREAM YOGA PRACTICES

• Practice concentration exercises to gain single-pointedness of mind.

• Watch your breath, thoughts, and emotions before sleep.

• Hold an object—a mala or stone or written prayer—throughout the night.

• Visualize yourself surrounded in a cocoon of Light as you go to sleep.

• Keep the Mantra as your last thought before falling asleep.

• Sleep on your left side closing your right nostril and breathing through your left nostril.

• Practice surrender and listening to the voice of the inner Guru.

EXERCISES AND REFLECTIONS

1. Find out how many repetitions it takes until you can say aloud a prayer or Mantra without any other intruding thought. One way to practice this is to close your eyes and recite the prayer, line by line. As soon as you have an intruding thought, open your eyes, and begin again. It is very important not to try to cheat yourself. Instead, just accept where you are at the moment and recognize that you have more work to do to increase concentration.

2. Daily diary writing and reflection become increasingly important. Ask yourself:

   What is dream?

   What is fantasy?

   What are emotional needs?

   What is my heart reflecting?

What do I reflect to other people?

Can I be a seed of inspiration to others?

Can I receive seeds of inspiration?

3. Dream Yoga is done in conjunction with sharpening sense perceptions for greater awareness—to hear with the inner ear, to smell, taste, see, touch the divine presence. Because dreams are very strongly influenced by your senses, it is very important to know precisely how your five senses function. The power of the senses needs to be carefully investigated.

Is that wonderful being you have seen in the eyes of the inner mind a fantasy? Wishful thinking? Or is it really a kind of divine presence?

If you smell roses and violets or sandalwood, what does it indicate? What insights arise?

When you have a dream in which you have been seeing, can you recall that dream again from the sense of hearing?

Recall the dream, each time from a different sense.

4. Observe the effects on your dreams as you practice the Dream Yoga exercises. It is necessary to go slowly, to assess your situation again and again, and to take careful note of your thoughts and feelings, and even of the physical aspect of sleeping in the prescribed position. Emotional reactions and moods need to be dealt with and carefully noted down to make the picture complete.

24

Confirming Dreams

AS YOU LEARN to concentrate on the Light and Mantra, and as you develop an attitude of surrender and total reliance on your dreams, you will find that dreams give you exactly what you need. It may take some time before you receive insights at the highest levels because if you have neglected your inner being, it takes time to re-establish contact. Be patient and remember that it takes nine months even to be born.

Eventually you will have wonderful dreams— dreams of divine guidance—confirmations, instructions, and inspirations. You might have an intense period where your dreams are very inspirational, but then at another time find that all inspiration suddenly vanishes for some years. In the interim, before the elevated dreams return, you will probably receive dreams of purification—"rinsing the mud off the Cadillac," as I sometimes call the process.

The more you truly want the divine contact and guidance and the more you can say thank you for even the smallest awareness or insights that arise, the more cooperation you will receive from your Higher Self. If you wait for some extraordinary vision of Lord Krishna, you can miss the sparkling little insights that have their own greatness. Even a small light can help us find our way; we do not always need a magnificent sunrise. Whenever you have an insight, take time to reflect on it. To help interpret your dreams you can practice what I call a "prayer without words" by sitting quietly in a receptive mood with your hands upturned in your lap. The position is your silent affirmation, "Whatever I am given, I want to understand."

Take every insight as a milestone on the Path of the Light. If there are long gaps between milestones, keep going nevertheless. Sometimes you can ask your dreams for a confirmation: "Please let me know if I am still going in the right direction." The confirmation will come.

I learned that I could depend on my dreams to tell me when I was doing the right thing and when I was not. Therefore I could take refuge in my dreams. I could completely rely on the inner Guru to respond to my needs.

What were my needs? I had no experience in running an ashram. I had spent only six months at Sivananda Ashram in India, and during that time I was concentrated on my spiritual development. I certainly did not receive instructions in administration, and what I did learn came from observing those in charge—listening to the intonation of their voices and watching the expression on their faces, because I did not speak the language.

So when I had established the ashram in Canada, as my Guru had requested, I was often very worried: "Am I making wise decisions? Am I handling problems correctly?" I wished that I could receive some indication that I was on the right track. I remember rushing to the front door whenever mail was delivered, unconsciously hoping for a letter that would answer all my questions—which, of course, could never come. My lack of experience was so great that my only hope was to surrender and to try to maintain contact with the Divine. I learned to rely totally on my dreams—and they proved to be very reliable indeed.

Prior to the following dream, which I had during the formative years of the ashram, one of the young residents had challenged me by saying that there were so many religious fanatics thinking they were doing the will of God, how did I know *I* was. Of course this was the very question I was agonizing over. I was still at the stage where I had many doubts about myself: "Am I really good enough? I know I don't have a pure mind—why should I have been chosen for the Divine Work?"

Then I had this dream.

Repairing the Road

I had to walk down a certain road. When I saw that it was very rough and difficult to walk upon, I decided to bring a tool with me. The tool looked something like a wooden snow shovel, and I used it to push the snow, mud, stones, and dirt to the right and left sides, out of the way. When I found some ice underneath, I turned the tool upside down since it had a steel point at the other end, and I broke the ice quite easily with it. As I worked, the road became clear and clean and easy to walk upon.

Suddenly I came upon a big hole right in the middle of the road. I stopped and filled it in, then tramped and stamped down the earth to make sure it was level with the rest. Now the road was smooth and anyone could go back and forth easily at any time.

I could have jumped over the hole, I thought, but then what would happen to others who might come along, especially in the dark?

The next morning the same young man who had challenged me asked if I had had a dream. He was usually very critical, but when I told him this dream I saw his eyes suddenly fill with tears. In a quiet voice he said he would not question again why I, a woman, had been chosen for the work. So the dream and the interaction that followed confirmed to me that I was doing the work appropriately. To me the road symbolized spiritual life, and the tool represented the spiritual tools I had been given. This particular tool was not a refined one—not something that required the precise skill of a jeweler—but it was the right tool for this job. With it I could clear the path of obstacles, making it easier for others to walk upon, and I could fill in the gaps that might otherwise be dangerous for those who would follow.

~

As we try to maintain contact with the Divine even in our sleep, our spiritual concepts take on a very definite form. In the following dream, I am again given a confirmation even as I express uncertainty about my ability.

Krishna's Flute

A messenger brought me a beautiful parcel wrapped in paper with little roses on it, and a pink ribbon. There was a card, "To Radha, my beloved."

The messenger said, "I am bringing this gift from Lord Krishna. Do you know who he is?"

"Yes, I know." I was overjoyed. Then I opened the parcel. It was a flute. "But I can't play the flute," I said.

Then the messenger asked, "Would you be given a flute if you couldn't play it?"

As human beings we are often beset with feelings of inferiority, or even sinfulness and inadequacy. My own Guru realized that not only women of the Orient, but women all over the world have had little chance to develop self-confidence and determination. That is why when Swami Sivananda initiated me, he said, "Put my name (Sivananda) in front of yours (Radha)." He knew this would give a boost to my self-esteem. When I told Swami Sivananda that I was not perfect enough or holy enough to establish an ashram in the West, he smiled and said, "Just be Lord Krishna's flute. Let the Divine play the melody. Learn to listen, and all will be well."

And now the flute had arrived!

Krishna's flute is a marvelous symbol. A bamboo flute is really just a stick with holes in it that cannot hold anything at all. If you pour water into it, the water will run out. And a flute cannot produce any music by itself. Krishna's flute can be heard only when the Divine gives the intuitive perception of its will, and we can surrender to it. Over the years I began to understand that while quick intellectual answers might pop into my mind, it was better to put them aside and wait for the voice of spiritual intuition to be heard.

Some time later, I had the same dream again but,

This time I took out the flute, played it immediately, and said, "The others will wonder at how well I can play."

The "others" were the people who gave me the sharpest criticism.

After having this dream of Krishna's flute, I understood that I needed to become an instrument through which the Divine could pour its melody. That meant not only listening intuitively, but being willing to say what was needed, even if the other person did not like it. If I was concerned about whether people liked me or not, I could not do the work, I could not play the flute. This was my experience and it is something that I can recall in an instant and remind myself, "Never mind—it doesn't matter if anybody likes me. Just be Lord Krishna's flute."

◡

The other saying that my Guru often used was "the milk of Divine Wisdom." He told me to be a spiritual mother to all, and that the mother has the milk before the baby is born. Somehow this symbolism penetrated my mind and became quite real in the following dream.

Feeding the Babies

A woman wearing many long skirts said to me, "There are many babies and they are very hungry. You should nourish them."

I said, "But I'm not a mother."

"Oh, don't make such a fuss," she said, and opened my blouse. She put one baby on each breast, saying, "You have two breasts. Put one here, the other there, and this bigger child can stand here and wait." He looked about two years old.

I was amazed that I would have milk to give. I looked over my shoulder, thinking the milk must come from somewhere else because I couldn't believe I would have any.

Then this same large woman came and took the first babies away. I saw the little two-year-old standing there, waiting, and behind him I suddenly saw that there was a whole army of people lined up, waiting—babies, children, and adults. I started to get up, thinking that I would be here forever, when two heavy hands pushed me back to my seat, and the enormous woman who was now standing behind me said, "You will sit here as long as I need you!"

Some people came with little buckets, and one person even had a frying pan.

The dream reassured me that I could do what my Guru had asked of me. Somehow—even though I could not understand how it was possible—the milk of Divine Wisdom was given. When I look back now, I see that there was, indeed, an army of people, spiritual babies of all sizes and shapes, passing through the ashram wanting to be nourished. But it was quite a strange experience having to sit there with this enormous being standing behind me and holding me down with her hands on my shoulders. It had an impact that I can hardly describe. There is no question of choice when Divine Mother wants us on the job.

Dreams like these gave me the strength to face the most formidable obstacles and the greatest challenges. Once I had the clear confirmation from the inner Guru that I was going in the right direction, it did not matter if people disagreed with my approach or found fault with my personality. I tried to please the Divine, not other people.

So dreams can give us a deep inner knowing that helps us to develop the strength we need to pursue the goal. When we place our trust in the Divine, we will certainly experience the influence of the Divine through our dreams.

EXERCISES AND REFLECTIONS

1. After writing down your dream, sit for a few moments in a receptive position palms upturned in your lap. Silently repeat the affirmation, "I want to understand whatever I have been given." Allow the interpretation of your dream to arise from within.

2. Review your dreams from the week and collect your insights, like precious gems. What light do they shed

on your life and direction at this time? Put your insights into action and find out what the results are.

3. Ask your dreams, "Am I doing the right thing?" Then, wait for the answer. Through your own experience you will gain trust in the inner Guru.

4. Ask yourself:

What are my needs at this time?

How do I distinguish between needs and desires?

How are my dreams responding to my real needs?

5. Find out if you have had dreams where your spiritual concepts take form. What is the message?

25

Instructive Dreams

*T*HE AREA OF the spirit is capable of transmitting quite a different kind of guidance to the human being in us through our intuition. As you work with your dreams you will discover that there is not just emotional meaning in dreams; there is also knowledge from other levels. That knowledge is available to us at all times, but we have to acquire a certain skill and we have to prepare to receive it. If I have a 15-watt bulb, I can expect only a dim light. If I want more light, I have to provide the lamp with a more powerful bulb—40-watt, 60-watt, 100-watt, 200-watt. But there is also a limitation to the lamp, which is only wired for so much. In the same way, we may be capable of handling only a limited amount of spiritual energy. Through a number of experiences, we have to become prepared to receive divine knowledge and to recognize its source.

When you take a prayerful attitude with a deep desire to know what you should do, you can receive explicit directions in no uncertain terms. I had several dreams in which I was given very direct instructions. The following dream shows just how straightforward and useful that advice can be—both for our own development and for helping others. A voice spoke directly to me, as follows.

Instructions

"You should first cut away the roots from the trees around you that have become intertwined with your own. They represent others' concepts that you have allowed to slip in. Watch for wrong acceptance of authority.

"You were shown in previous dreams that you have great wealth. What makes you think you should just keep it in your purse? Stop being afraid that you will create karma. Take a one-dollar bill at a time, break it into change, and start with the coins. But do something with it. What is not put to use is taken away.

"Do not worry about making mistakes. Remember, Divine Grace is always available to those who do the Divine Work. Keep watching your dreams—they will show you when something is wrong, truly wrong. But you will sail in big storms without a drop of water spilling into your boat, so there is no need to worry.

"Talk to people mentally if you cannot reach them otherwise. You can start by sitting quietly by yourself and

*talking in your own mind to that ill woman you are con-
cerned about, at the same time wrapping her in Light.
This will help remove the garbage from her unconscious.
Every little clearing will bring her great relief. Do this
with everyone you wish to help. In this way you will first
light a candle in their unconscious. In time, as they get
used to the Light, you can increase its strength.*

*"You must understand that many tools are needed si-
multaneously—a coarse broom for the coarse dirt, a fine
broom for the dust. You must get all your tools in proper
working order, which means developing your powers of
mind. When you are given a new tool, add it to what you
have been given. Otherwise you are like a child who, when
given one toy, forgets about all the others.*

"Work is expected from you now and a good output."

So when we ask to have our dream messages
straight, we will get them straight. Who was the sender
of the message? I have considered different possibilities.
I could say the inner Guru or the Higher Self. If consciousness can survive after a physical being has disappeared, I could speculate that it was the consciousness
of another that was influencing me through the dream.
Perhaps the message was a reflection of my own past
knowledge being transmitted. There was no doubt that
the words were wise.

Cutting away roots meant taking responsibility for
my own ideas and clearing out those concepts that had
become entangled with mine through conditioning. So
I started uprooting ideas that were based on culture,
education, social status, tradition. I struggled to free
myself from the values of the family—traditional ideas

about what was good and bad, which were based only on social rules and had nothing to do with the spiritual path. I discovered in which areas I was imitating my mother, my grandmother, and my teachers. Many of their ideas were not really my convictions, so why should I continue to carry them? As I worked with freeing my roots, I had a sense of breathing more easily.

When I began to observe those people whom I had considered very holy and knowledgeable, I started to see that some of them could talk wonderfully about spiritual ideas, but they did not put their words into practice in their lives. It took me quite some time to recognize how I had accepted false authority, probably because I had been looking for encouragement and wanted others to do what I could not yet do.

The fear of making mistakes and creating karma had sometimes crippled my ability to take action. In the early years of my spiritual life I felt I did not have enough discrimination to act wisely. But I had to *learn* to make decisions, which is why my Guru did not respond to the specific questions in my letters. This fear of creating karma followed me around for a long time because I had become so aware of my thoughts. I was overly anxious about every wrong thought, every wrong action, and worrying about how I could have let them happen. "Do not worry about making mistakes," was an important lesson for me to learn. Now from my own experience, I give people in new positions the same advice: "Don't worry if you make mistakes—it is bound to happen. We learn by trial and error."

This dream gave me invaluable instructions about the best way to help certain people. When I practiced the suggested method I found that when my intensity was strong enough, the prayers, mental conversation, and Light would have results. The prayers and Light could take people out of their regular patterns and lift them to quite a different, much higher level. But if the person who was meant to receive the Light had even stronger resistance, then there was nothing more I could do.

"Keep watching your dreams—they will show you when something is wrong, truly wrong."

Here was a dream telling me that I could depend on my dreams. When we can listen, when we can free ourselves of the prisons created by a sense of personal inadequacy, fear of criticism and rejection, then we begin to clear the way for the messages from a greater reality to come through.

And we can ask, "What are the realities of the dreaming mind?"

EXERCISES AND REFLECTIONS

1. Review your dreams to discover instructive dreams. You cannot receive this kind of dream until you learn to listen. If you cannot listen in waking life, how can you hear the voice of the inner Guru in dreams? Practice listening in daily life.[1]

2. Are you sincerely seeking directions? Would you follow the instructions given to you by your inner Guru?

When I was asking myself, "How would I know the will of God? How would I know whether or not I

[1] See Radha, *Kundalini,* for exercises to develop the ability to listen.

could surrender to that will?" I realized that it was imperative to have some way of knowing, since my Guru was so far away that he could not provide direct guidance. I decided I would do a surrender practice. I chose a very critical person from my environment, put that person into the Light for a week, and at the end of the week followed every suggestion, order, or demand the individual made during the next week. I gradually extended the surrender practice to two weeks, three weeks, and finally three months. I made it clear to myself before I started that I would not do anything that would go against my conscience, but I would not let any financial expenses stand in the way of surrender.

If you decide to try this practice, notice your responses and reactions. They will show you where self-will is active. This process exercises your ability to surrender to the Divine.

3. To have direct dreams you have to overcome pride and be willing to admit your mistakes. Pray for the courage to look at things straight on and the strength to deal with what comes up. If you are earnest in your request, direct dreams will come. They can save you a great deal of time.

4. Make a conscious effort in your waking state to set your conscious mind aside and listen to the voice of intuition. If you want to discover and develop this reflective mode in yourself, observe the transition time of dusk or dawn. Then ask yourself:

What is the dawn or the dusk of my mind?

What keeps me from being in that twilight space?

26

Dream Experiences

WHEN YOU ARE already working with your psychological problems and you are sincerely willing to learn, then you can be given spiritual food. I make a distinction between dreams in the usual sense that have a psychological meaning, and dreams that I call "experiences" because a different part of consciousness is present. "Dream experiences" are different from ordinary dreams because they go beyond the individual's mind to a greater source where wisdom is contacted and instruction is received. Dream experiences have a tremendous impact on how you live your life afterwards.

When you first have a small experience—an insight like a flash of awareness—if you invoke a feeling of gratitude, many more flashes of awareness will come. It is as if I ask you for a favor, and when you respond very nicely, I thank you sincerely. Then you will be willing to help me again. If your ego just brushes the experience off, it may not return. Treat your own Higher Self in the same way. Give it power to come into the foreground. It will exercise its power in a most beneficial way.

Dreams can prepare you for a little more, and then a little more. But if you do not pay attention to your insights, including your hunches, and if you take everything for granted, one of two things can happen: intuition may disappear entirely for the rest of your life, or you may experience a strong force from your Higher Self that pushes your objections and callousness aside and says, "Listen. Now *pay attention!*" Then you can have an extraordinary experience.

The following dream, "Solitary Confinement," was almost like a telepathic contact that gave me vital instructions for my spiritual development.

Solitary Confinement

I entered a big building, which I realized was a prison. People were sitting at long tables, very focused on what they had right in front of them, looking down, bent over. Then the prison warden asked me, "Would you like to go to the upper levels where the prisoners are in solitary confinement?"

"Yes," I said. Then I asked him, "Do these people know they are in prison?"

"No, and they are quite happy with what they are doing. They are captivated by it. That's all they focus on."

I felt very astonished at this. Is it possible that people are in prison and don't even know it? I could hardly get over it. Not only did they seem to be unaware of where they were, but they were also apparently happy.

We went up to another level, where the more dangerous prisoners were kept in solitary confinement. There was one man in particular whom I noticed in a cell like a small cage. On the wall was a very straight bed with a simple blanket where he was sitting in a perfect lotus posture with his eyes closed. I stood quietly and watched him. He looked peaceful.

After a little while he opened his eyes, and I asked, "Do you know that you are in prison?"

"Yes," he said.

"Do you have to work here?"

"A little."

"What else do you do?"

"I leave the prison. I go somewhere else."

"Where do you go?"

"To places of great knowledge. And because of this freedom I do not mind being here, as there is always time to do what is important after I have done what is requested of me."

"But how do you get out?" The walls of the prison were bare concrete.

"Oh, I just sit here quietly and 'think' my way out," he explained to me. "The guard knows to some extent that he is in prison. All the others in the big hall down below don't know. But I can think my way out. I leave my body

and come back without anyone knowing. Only in solitary confinement are we free."

I was rather puzzled by that.

"Not even the warden knows of my freedom," he added.

I looked at the warden-guide. He seemed absent-minded. His face was somehow "clouded." I was speechless, amazed, and shaken.

"Do you read books?" I asked when my voice came back. "Do you study metaphysical books?"

He said he read a little and that there was some stimulation in books, but all that mattered was thinking through and thinking one's way out!

"Are there other prisoners in solitary confinement?"

"Yes," he nodded. "Some do the same. Some have not yet reached the same freedom."

I felt my mind working at tremendous speed. Finally I got hold of the thought that seemed to be paramount. Where was this prison? The world? The body? The mind? The ashram?

He smiled again. It put me at ease. "Ashram and world are the same. Therefore the prison is the body and the mind. It is good that you see the prison walls where they are. That is the first step to freedom."

He stretched out his hand to me. I took it with both of mine.

"Solitary confinement! Solitary confinement!" With those words I awoke.

I immediately understood that the ground floor of the prison represented ordinary life. Most people do not know they are in a prison. They are under the illu-

sion that life is great and gives them what they want. When I first started asking people what the purpose of their life was, they would give me blank looks and say, "What a strange question! I have my family, my children, my work." They were prisoners who did not know that they were in prison—the prison of their ideas, the prison of their concepts, and especially the prison of their concept of what life was about. The dream assured me that there was no need to be concerned about those who did not yet know that they were in prison, because others, "the wardens," would take care of them.

Stimulation in small quantities—carefully selected books—seemed to be all right if thinking stayed the main work—thinking things through and thinking my way out. Thoughts have to be directed. I had recognized early in my life that undirected thoughts had a negative influence on my physical well-being and my psychic strength. I had noticed that ambitious businessmen, despite pressure from all sides, often seemed less tired than people who allowed their thoughts to roam, even if their bodies were quite relaxed.

"Only in solitary confinement are we free." Only in self-imposed solitary confinement can we think our way out of our prisons. Solitary confinement to most people is probably the worst condition imaginable, and those who have experienced it—people held hostage, for example— say they were afraid of losing their minds. But I knew that solitary confinement could have other possibilities.

Solitary confinement could mean being isolated from all influences that can manipulate the mind, being isolated from all influences from the senses. So when all these influences and manipulations are gone, an incredible power can be released that can work for the Divine and overcome many obstacles. To make contact with something else within ourselves, which we can call the Divine or the Guru within, we need to confine ourselves to solitude, to quietness, to meditation. Then when the inner Guru takes over, it can present new realities to us through dreams and experiences.

The prisoner in the dream experience had an incredible freedom. He would just sit, close his eyes, and leave his body. He could go to places of great knowledge. Nobody knew he had gone. What was it then that leaves? The spiritual spark? If it could leave and go to another area or if it could offer help to others, then perhaps I, too, could do this if I put myself into the Light. I practiced this for years, saying, "This physical house is protected in the spiral of Light. Now something else— my soul or inner Light, the vortex of energy that we call 'consciousness'—can do the other work where the body cannot go." Eventually I received confirmation that this was indeed so.

I learned that consciousness does not have to take the body along. And the fact that when you "wake up," you find yourself in the chair where you were meditating or the bed where you were sleeping does not mean that you have to dismiss such an experience as a hallucination. If we sit outside and suddenly smell the perfume of flowers coming to us, we have not gone to the flower and the flower has not come to us. The perfume is invisible. We cannot see how it travels; but if we have a certain sensitivity, we can become aware of that perfume. It is similar with these experiences. It is the spark of life's essence that is able to move freely. What we bring along is that vortex of energy which is not necessarily visible to the senses.

Some time later the same dream experience recurred—the same prison, the same guard, the same prisoner in solitary confinement.

You Must Kill!

This time I asked him, "Would I have to <u>commit</u> something in order to be sentenced to solitary confinement?"

"Exactly," he responded.

"Why did you get solitary confinement?"

"I killed."

"Oh my God!"

And he said, "One day you will have to kill."

"No, I can't do this. Do I <u>have</u> to kill?"

"Yes."

"There is no other way?"

"No."

Then he looked at me and asked, "Do you know <u>what</u> you have to kill?"

And in the dream I knew. I had to kill the part of my mind that constantly creates and produces desires.

I have to kill the scheming of the mind. How would I go about that? The answer was really in the Bhagavad Gita.[1] All the power of desires had to be brought together and focused entirely on the Divine. Then I had

---

[1] Bhagavad Gita, Text and Commentary by Swami Sivananda (Durban, South Africa: Sivananda Press, 1968).

to accept that the Divine gives, the Divine takes away. I would not say, "Oh wonderful! I am so happy to have been given this or that!" Or, "How terrible! Look at all my losses!" I had to find the place in the middle and be able to say, "I shall neither be overjoyed, nor will I cry. Some things are wonderful and I can appreciate them as long as I have them, but if the Divine wants them, I will give them back. Life is given, the opportunity to serve the Divine is given, and though my desire is great, I will come home only when I have fulfilled my promise."

EXERCISES AND REFLECTIONS

1. You need to find time to extract yourself from daily life, to confine yourself to going within, to meditation. It is in solitude that the opening happens. If I knock on your door long enough and intensely enough, you will open it. The Guru within will not even keep you waiting that long.

    In solitude, you can intensify your awareness in spiritual practices. Reflect on what each line of the Divine Light Mantra really means to you. Observe what actually happens when you chant a Mantra. Become aware of the vibrations in the body and the effects of the vibrations on the mind.

2. Continue the practice of wrapping yourself in Light before you go to sleep, "protecting the house, the physical body."

27

Substantiation of Spiritual Dreams

W E CANNOT ALWAYS be sure when dreams come from a higher source, so we have to be cautious in our conclusions. If a dream is very positive it is easy to assume that it is a divine message. But each of us has many voices—the inner voices of our personality aspects—and if you do not know all your personality aspects, it is not so easy to determine which voice is the Higher Self. Anxiety, jealousy, temptation, admiration—all have voices. Which is which? After many years of working with my dreams, I am still extremely careful because I know the tricks of the mind.

You will need to investigate how many voices you have. In this process it is important that you do not judge or blame yourself. Simply learn to distinguish between the voices of your different personality aspects. Then keep careful records of your dreams, write them down, and if you act on a dream that you think is from a higher source, find out if the results of your actions measure up to the dream. How does the dream influence your behavior? If the dream was empowered by the ego, you may feel compelled to assert yourself. But if the influence was from the Divine, you will function from true devotion, humility, and sincerity. Do not ever assume that you "have arrived" and that you no longer need to work on yourself.

When you have a dream or visionary experience of the Divine, you need to know whether the mind has manufactured it or whether it is a true experience. If you have a very elated feeling, and if you cannot reproduce the experience again by your own imagination, you have two clues. You can repeat experiences created by your own imagination, but the real experiences and that feeling of elation you cannot repeat. Yet, when the mind is in what I call the "twilight state," an in-between state where it is open and receptive but also suggestible, you still have to ask, "How do I know for sure?"

Ask whether the dream is spiritual, and then wait until you receive a confirmation or substantiation. Substantiation is not absolute proof—there is no absolute proof. Dreams cannot be repeated like scientific experiments. But if you receive something tangible related to the dream, you have evidence that is at least convincing to your own mind. You may dream that a particular gift is coming your way. Though you are not able to perceive the source of the gift, you may feel it is from a higher level. If you eventually receive that gift in waking life, the dream is substantiated and you have the best evidence that the mind did not create a fantasy out of its own tremendous need for survival. Once the survival level is left behind, dreams can be incredibly instructive—helping you to open the door to the Divine within, helping you to find the entrance to your Cathedral of Consciousness.

Not every dream needs to be substantiated, but enough do so that you can tell the difference between an intense dream that was empowered by the ego, and one that was truly influenced by the Divine. I wait and see. I have often been given pieces of jewelry, which I think of as "spiritual jewelry" because they served to confirm or verify certain dream experiences.

After I had returned to Canada from India, I was sending monthly reports to my Guru and asking for his advice, but I never received further instructions. At the time I wanted to know if I was doing things correctly, and when I did not receive an answer I became quite discouraged. But one night I had this dream.

The First To Come

A very blond child came to me with a whole handful of jewelry and said, "This is all waiting for you, and you will get these one by one." He held out a ring to me and said, "This will be the first to come."

I looked at the ring, and I felt partly surprised, partly overjoyed, and partly shocked. The ring was in the design of a crusader's cross, and I had no desire to be either a cru-

sader or a missionary. I did not think in terms of fulfilling my mission in life.

Some time later, under most unusual circumstances, a diamond ring set in the form of a crusader's cross was given to me.[1] The experience assured me that signs confirming our progress on the spiritual path do come. The ring was a substantiation of the dream.

I never asked for a substantiation of the dream, but it happened. This and other substantiations confirmed the reality that otherwise would have been hard for me to accept—the kinds of dreams that seemed too good to be true. For me, having a material manifestation—something that remained visible—was enough evidence that these special dream experiences had an undeniable reality. We have already examined the power of wishful thinking and know that a desire, when combined with strong emotions, may eventually manifest. But some manifestations have little to do with the limited powers of our own minds.

To show you what I mean, I will give you a detailed example of a dream experience and how it was substantiated.

The Two Chariots

I cannot describe the place I'm at, but several crates are being delivered to me. The first crate opens itself somehow to reveal a beautiful golden chariot. Fantastic! I am tremendously impressed by it and very excited. At the same time, I am aware of the dream's importance and feel a sense of urgency to remember it and write it down.

---

[1] See Radha, *Divine Light Invocation,* 53-55.

The entire chariot is pure gold and emerges from the crate all in one piece. I run my fingers along the design on the side. It is like a piece of jewelry—extraordinary, beautiful—reflecting the light with a soft glow. Then I see another person, who gestures for me to come to the other side of the chariot. As I walk around it I see flashes of blue light, and there, on the back of one of the seats I see, written in dazzling blue sapphires, R-A-D-H-A. The second seat is unmarked. I am stunned. I think, "It could only be Lord Krishna's chariot!"

At this point, my feeling of urgency wakes me, and I repeat the dream to myself with a feeling of surprise and tremendous joy, realizing that the Divine will not let me down. Despite the many problems over the years, the Divine will always keep its promise—this is the message. After I write down the dream, I remember the other crates and feel I must find out what they contain. Very brief images of Radha and Krishna flit through my mind as I lie down again. Then the full scene reappears, without losing any detail.

The golden chariot is still there for me to see. And now I am given help in opening the other crates. I see pieces of beautifully carved sandalwood, which I realize will form another chariot—a bigger one—when the pieces are all put together. There are many pieces and it may take quite some time to fit them all together so that the chariot can be used. The carvings are of the finest quality, very intricate and delicate.

*I have the feeling, "These carvings are too exquis-
ite to be burned." I also have the thought, "But
there are no horses. The chariot is Krishna's
chariot; and there is my name, RADHA, but there
are no horses." Then a voice says, "The horses will
be here when the time comes."*

When I wake up again, a question appears in my
mind: "When will I ride in the golden chariot, and when
will I ride in the wooden carved one?" The golden
chariot must be the vehicle of my Higher Self, to carry
it home. The wooden chariot is, perhaps, the body. One
day it will burn, because I have always wanted my body
to be cremated. The body will be taken in a vehicle to
the crematorium long after the golden chariot has disappeared with the essence of Radha.

Yes, I could understand that. The body is a vehicle.
Sylvia is a vehicle for that particular ray of Light called
Radha.[2] That the chariot had to be put together was true,
because my body had suffered and needed to heal. The
various parts of my body had to function better so the
body could work better as a whole. But I felt it was also
quite possible that the pieces of the chariot could refer
to my notes and writings, those insights and inspirations which I had jotted down over the years in the hope
that I would have time to put them together one day.
Although the dream announced that the golden chariot
was here, it also said the wooden chariot still has to be

---

[2] "Sylvia" was my name before initiation. I sometimes use my two
names—Sylvia and Radha—to show that both the human and divine aspects coexist in us.

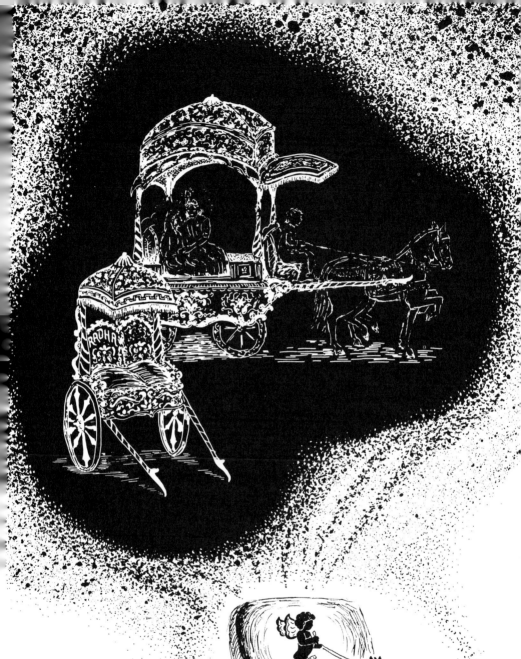

assembled. This made me realize that I might have to resign myself to living longer, until the job was done.

Still the message of the dream was so extraordinary, so promising. I wanted to be sure that I was not tricking myself by strong, wishful thinking—even if it came from my heart—so I said to myself, "This dream seems too good to be true. I can hardly believe it. The golden chariot is like a piece of jewelry. If I ever see a piece of jewelry like this chariot, then I will really accept the dream as a message from the Divine." But, I thought, "Who would ever make a piece of jewelry in the shape of a chariot, and if somebody did make it, who would wear it?"

Some years earlier, a student of mine had been talking to me about a career change. We had tossed around all kinds of ideas, and he had talked about his interests and mentioned that somebody in his family was in the jewelry business, which quite intrigued him. One day I was at an antique store and I happened to see a pamphlet on courses offered in gemology, so I picked one up and gave it to him. He was delighted, and immediately started taking courses in antique jewelry.

He went really enthusiastically into his research. He talked to other people in the business, took courses in both business and gems, bought a number of books on diamonds and semi-precious stones and equipment, and went to exhibits. He was very interested and loved to talk about it. One weekend, he went to a wonderful exhibition of antique jewelry. At the close of the exhibition he was trying to decide whether or not to pick up one of their catalogues for an auction being held in Toronto. The catalogues were quite expensive and he would be unable to attend the auction, so in some ways it did not make sense. But he thought it over, and when he saw that the one in front of him was the last one, he decided to purchase it.

When he showed me the catalogue, he said, "This is all antique jewelry, and I'll bet I know your taste so well that I could point out exactly what you would like." So we sat together and enjoyed leafing through the book.

And suddenly—there it was! A tiny, exquisitely crafted gold brooch in the form of a chariot. I was so enchanted by it that my friend immediately asked if he could give it to me as a gift, and though the auction was in Toronto and he was on the West Coast, he managed to put in his bid and successfully purchase this very special piece. He phoned me to say, "Your golden chariot is on the way." This time the chariot arrived not in a crate, but in a tiny parcel.

What could I do now? Could I say my dream was a fantasy? A desire? Only my imagination? No. But what *must* I say? That my obligation to Krishna should be a thousand-fold more, because the symbol was a tangible confirmation of the dream's reality.

By the way, shortly after this, my friend completely lost interest in the jewelry business. In fact, when I told him the whole story, he laughingly said that the Divine had used him for its own ends.

～

This kind of substantiation happened not just with this one piece of jewelry, but with many pieces—so many that the first dream of the little boy showing me the jewelry and saying I would receive each piece, one by one, has been realized.

I wonder if the people who have given me these lovely gifts realize that they have been messengers of the Divine. For me the gifts were especially precious because they had come from friends who were attracted to the teachings and understood what I was doing. If these people remember having been the messengers of the Divine, perhaps that thought will give them enough support in their own struggles that they, in turn, can inspire others.

When you have concrete evidence that your dream has a level of reality beyond the psychological, you can ask yourself, "What was different about this dream? How did I feel? How did the dream come about?" When you recognize the pattern, you can wait for its recurrence. After you have had a number of similar experiences and they have been substantiated, you really know that you can receive messages from the Divine through your dreams.

But the more you try to understand before you experience, the less you will ever truly experience. You can only experience first and then try to explain it later, and most of the time even that explanation does not work. Whatever comes from the Divine should be received as a gift. I have not tried to use my intellect to find a reason why it has come—that would be like taking the gift apart to see how good it is on the inside. It is better to allow feelings of gratitude and awe to well up for what the Divine is and gives than to want an explanation.

There will come a time when we no longer need any confirmations, when we recognize and trust the divine messages. But it is very good not to stop questioning too soon. Because again and again I have seen how tricky the mind can be and how it can create so much out of a survival need.

It has become perfectly clear to me that when we pick up the clues and put them all together, we will find quite a number of messages from the Divine. We are never really left without confirmations if we are just more attentive and if we do not take any gift for granted.

EXERCISES AND REFLECTIONS

1. The practice of returning to a particular dream to carry the dream into waking consciousness is a very important one. Do you ever have dreams where you dream a bit, wake up, and then go back and continue the dream? It is like reading a book. You lay the book aside and when you come back to it, you go over the last paragraph you read and then continue from there.

2. Get to know your personality aspects and their different voices. You can observe them in your everyday interactions. Make a list of them. You can even give them names. Become familiar enough with them that you can distinguish which personality aspects speak in the dream.

3. If you have a dream that you think is from a higher source, observe how the dream influences your behavior. Dream experiences have a dramatic impact on your life. See also if the dream is substantiated in the particular way in which you can recognize and accept it.

28

The Promise: Mystical Union

HE MOMENTS WHEN we rise above the whole bundle of our personalities and really function through our essence are extremely rare. It is a rare moment when we really act out of love for the Divine. Such moments express what I call "a love affair with the Divine." In dreams and mythology this love between the devotee and the Divine is often represented by a marriage or union. There is nothing that compares to it. Through very special, inspiring dreams we can be lifted out of ourselves to experience this Divine Love. These special dream experiences are what some people may call "visions" or "spiritual experiences." They are really meditative experiences that occur in a state when the conscious mind is not active.

Perhaps there truly is no other love than Divine Love. The human love we seek is an illusion—the fulfillment of the concept that each one of us has about love. But the Divine almost constantly has to overlook all our faults, mistakes, shortcomings, broken promises, broken intentions, and human weaknesses. We can be very scattered in our approach to the Divine or very rigid. If we are regular and persistent in our practices, we can become routine and lose depth. Yet if we do not persist and do not pursue our goal, our intentions are like sparks flashing here and there, coming to nothing. Yet still Divine Love is there.

We cannot love the Divine in the same way that we love an object or another person. With the Divine you feel happy that after all you have been through, you have finally made your way back again. Certainly you are aware of how long you have been away—the time of separation—and you feel joyfully ecstatic to be back.

The only permanent love is love from the Divine— even when you do not recognize it, even when you feel separated. As long as you do not turn away, the Divine is facing you all the time. The Divine does not turn away. The sun does not disappear from the sky when it is covered by clouds. Divine Light is covered only by the clouds of your own thinking and your own emotions, and when the Light breaks through the clouds it is like consciousness breaking through to another dimension.

I would not claim even today to know what love is. Is a powerful commitment love itself? That could be. If commitment to the Divine is an expression of love for the Divine, then the protection from the Divine is an expression of love from the Divine. I can see the interdependence: the human depends on the Divine and yet the Divine also depends on the human form, the human voice, and human love to convey and manifest Divine Love.

I have found that the divinity within ourselves will respond to what we need on the human level because that human aspect also needs nourishment. The obstacle is often that we feel we are too bad or too sinful to accept our own divinity, and if we do accept the Divine within, it is almost dangerous to acknowledge it to anybody else because it will be interpreted as ego. We have to watch, too, that our own human nature does not try to destroy out of jealousy whatever the Divine produces or the emerging divine spark. Doubts can be a kind of attack, a war that the mind has with our own divine nature.

When I needed help to keep me going spiritually, I had a series of dreams. These experiences, which were more than dreams, were needed to balance the challenges I was facing in my daily life. This series came cloaked in Christian symbolism, probably influenced by my retreat and meditation on the book of Revelation and its relation to the Kundalini system. For many years of my life the Pope had appeared in books and magazines as a symbol of the Divine. The Pope is said to walk in the shoes of Peter and to be the representative of Jesus on earth. I probably accepted this at one time and incorporated it into my personal symbolism.

The dream series which follows is an example of consciousness breaking through to another dimension.

Recalling such significant dreams is extremely important, even though memory is not the actual experience.
If I eat a piece of fruit or drink a glass of wine, later I
can only remember the experience; that remembering
is not the experience itself. What is stirred in the memory
is the effect, the reflection, the echo, of what the actual
experience of eating the fruit or drinking the wine created in me.

If I awaken the memory of remarkable dreams and
experiences by going through my diary, excerpting these
special events and reflecting on them, I can bring back
to life that which responded in me at the time. Naturally with dream experiences and experiences of the
Light, the effect is much greater than the memory of a
pleasant taste on the tongue.

Another way to increase your ability to receive spiritual dreams is to say thank you to your Higher Self. Give
that recognition to the source of the dream. Do not take
its gifts for granted. I understood from the beginning
that we cannot take even the most beautiful insight,
dream, inspiration, or vision to mean that now we can
take our spiritual evolution for granted, without making any further efforts. At no point in life, and probably
not in the afterlife either, can we take anything for
granted. That is probably the greatest mistake we can
make—taking each other for granted and taking the
Divine for granted.

Receiving the Mantle

*I find myself in a church of exquisite beauty. A very special
service is going on, and I wonder what the meaning of
this service is. There are a great number of dignitaries and*

only a few ordinary people like myself. I am in the back of the big room, but somehow I can still see everything quite well. I am not entirely unfamiliar with the service in a Catholic Church, but this Mass is all in Latin, which I do not understand, so I follow only what I recognize: the offerings.

Then each of these great men in their beautiful robes is handed a piece of paper on which they quickly write something. The papers are then collected in a large bowl before the altar. One priest leads a prayer and all chant a hymn. The same priest takes three papers from the bowl. Then an official, wearing a red robe with a white lace collar, comes over to me.

I feel terribly embarrassed. "Gosh, I should not be here. I am discovered at their very special service. Somebody will get in trouble for having overlooked the presence of a stranger." The priest asks me to step forward to receive my mantle. I don't know what to do.

I whisper, "But it is all a mistake. I should not be here. I am sorry to disturb you. I assure you, I did not mean to."

He looks at me sternly saying, "Will you please come to the altar to receive your mantle. It is the Lord's decision."

So I get up and follow him, hoping for the best. The mantle is a pearl gray color and I am given a black top hat to put on. Then I am told I have fifteen minutes before my speech. I go back to my place. I can't think. My mind rattles like an old car motor, the wheels turn wildly. When I discover that all eyes are on me, I decide to go to the washroom to be alone and think clearly for a few minutes about my speech. I am sure God will help me.

When I am in the washroom, I hear someone opening the door behind me. I step into the little booth but I
can't close the door because there is nothing to close it
with. The person passes by. "Goodness, it is the Pope! He
sees me. Am I in the men's room? Well, I'll have to make
the best of it." I walk out, bowing reverently to him and
trying to assume the best attitude I can—heart, mind,
and soul. I will just explain to him that I am not Catholic.

But he doesn't let me. Instead, he takes my arm and
firmly motions me out and back to the big church room.
As we walk up the steps, I dare to interrupt him with a very
personal remark. I say, "I know you are the Pope but I
don't even know how to address you. See! You have the
wrong person."

"I am called the Holy Father, you see, and you will be
given your name as soon as we arrive," he replies. He ca-
resses my arm with gentleness, and looks at me with a
deep and great expression of love.

It takes my last scrap of courage to say, "Holy Father, I
am not a Catholic, don't you understand? I intruded into
your church. You selected me in all ignorance of my
status as a stranger. I am terribly sorry to cause you
this inconvenience."

"Never mind about being a stranger. We, the holy
Church and I and its Founder, Jesus' follower"—he
points to a figure of Jesus— "believe in this ceremony, and
that God alone makes this decision. Don't worry about
not being Catholic. We will see to that." A moment of silence. "I, myself, shall baptize you. I, myself, shall receive
you into His arms. Now let us go."

So we go. We come to the church door. I try to open it
for the Holy Father but he doesn't let me. "Not today," he

whispers as he opens the door. All present look at us. They rise. The Pope walks to the altar. I stay behind, waiting his bidding. Someone offers me his chair. I sit down. A lovely high-sounding bell rings, like crystal when tapped with a silver spoon. I know my time has come.

My heart beats furiously. I keep walking, reach the chair of the Pope, and kneel down. A choir starts singing. But I can clearly hear the Pope saying, while laying his hands on my head, "Repeat: 'I am of lowly birth, lowly action, lowly speech. But by Thy grace I shall now lay all that I am at Thy feet. I have now received your mercy. I have received a new coat and a new name. I shall do all work in His name with His power.'"

I feel so shaken, I can hardly keep on my knees.

"Open your mouth," the Pope says. I do. He places the host into it and puts a glass with red wine on my lips.

The coolness of the glass is still with me.

I hear someone coming. Oh, they are coming to the Prayer Room. Good—then I am behind this great altar in the church. I am now with the Pope. Oh no, it's Kootenay Bay.[1] Someone is coming to sing Mantras. Wonderful. It's time, then, to get up. What a dream. My heart is still beating. My body feels sweaty. But I have to write down the dream first. I will feel better.

Now that the dream is on paper, my mind runs wild again. Previous dreams rush into my mind—the Upper Room where someone will meet me, my childhood experience playing with little angels, the Ave Maria. Then I begin to think,

---

[1] Kootenay Bay is where Yasodhara Ashram is located.

"But I have become a sanyasin, why would I dream in Christian symbolism?" Other experiences with the Buddha, with Divine Mother, with Krishna rush into my mind. How does this all fit together? A memory arises of one of the more advanced Kundalini exercises—visualizing the lotus at the base of the spine, first closed and then slowly opening. In the center of the lotus is a diamond of many facets. Divine power has many facets. It will use whatever shape, form, and color necessary to communicate itself. God is one; divine names are many.

With this thought I enter a peaceful meditation.

A few nights later, I had the following dream.

In the Garden

I am in a beautiful garden where many different types of flowers are in full bloom. As I walk along a sunlit path, I meet the Pope again. We walk together, hand in hand, and talk in a very friendly way about great and wonderful teachings. He explains many things to me. I am amazed at his wisdom and feel extremely happy—a happiness that I had never dreamed was possible. Every now and then I remember that the Pope walks in the shoes of Jesus, and I cannot wonder enough about how privileged I am to be with him. I silently promise myself to stay on this Path of Light, which is like a taste of Heaven.

When I look around at the amazing variety of flowers and trees, it becomes even clearer to me that while

God is one and without gender, the same creative force has expressed itself in an incredible multitude of ways—too vast ever to be grasped by the limitations of a human mind.

If we recognize the preciousness and the many facets in the many religions, if we stay focused on the beauty, the Light, and the wisdom that all religions have in common, then we can truly be a family of the Divine, and see ourselves as the creation of this Divine Cosmic Energy.

The third dream in this continuing series occurred several nights later.

The Wedding Awaits

I hear one of the young disciples calling outside my cabin, "Swamijiiii," several times. And as he comes closer his voice sounds louder. Then with a big bang he opens the door, still calling so loudly that it feels as if the roof will come down, "Swamijiiii!"

"What is it?" I ask him.

"They are all waiting for you. Hurry. Hurry. The Wedding. The Pope is already there!" Suddenly he looks at me and says, "Oh, that is beautiful! How beautiful, Swamiji! You must wear this always."

Now I look at myself and am just as surprised as he is. My body is transparent Light—I have no real dress but no real body, either. I am in a daze and go out and up the hill where the Cathedral is. The doors are wide open, and as I approach I hear lovely music—like organ music and like a choir of angels chanting.

Then I stand at the door. The sight is so overpowering I cannot move—not one single step. The big room where I

had received my mantle is already of such exquisite beauty, there are just no words to describe it. I see the Pope sitting on a throne in fantastic splendor—an unthinkable splendor, and yet here it is. I am so overwhelmed, almost paralyzed, that I go to the lake, sit down, and cry in sheer joy.

It is the Wedding—the Union between the Divine and me—so unthinkable and yet true. It seems too much to accept. I feel I've had my reward already, just knowing, even if the doors are closed again. If I walk up now to enter, the opportunity alone—my God, oh, my God—what great wonders ...

> *The first dream with the Pope: meeting the soul or Higher Self. The second dream with the Pope in the beautiful gardens: getting last instructions. Now comes the long awaited Wedding—the Union—and a new view—seeing things in their true perspective. This is a new experience of humility of quite an unknown quality. It is a joy at the same time. Even this glimpse of the Reality— the only one there is—is enough. This experience is an incentive. It will be the source of strength for whatever may come. The stage for the last drama is already set. It is now up to me to do the rest.*

In this final dream I had to make a decision. Should I stay here or should I go now? I knew if I entered the Cathedral, that would be the end of my life. In the dream I went to the lake to reflect. When a certain state of Realization is reached, the body falls away between nine and twenty-one days afterwards, and it will only stay on longer if you have a particular job to do. I felt a temptation to go, but I knew I had to keep my promise.

Out of this experience I received a powerful insight into the different temptations of the Buddha and Jesus. Jesus' temptation was the world, so he overcame it by teaching for only three years. The Buddha's temptation was what we call "heaven," and he overcame this by staying on earth to help people. The biggest difficulty for me after these dreams was to keep working and functioning on the ordinary three-dimensional level. I became so transparent and sensitive that life around me was almost unbearable. I would think, "I am not waiting for anything, I am not looking for anything, I have no unfulfilled desires. Why don't I go?"

I understood that the spiritual world is one world, but that does not mean that everything in the physical world is influenced in the way we would hope or expect. On earth the river flows downward; it is only in heaven where the river can flow upward. The mystical tree is rooted in heaven, where it can get nourishment and then grow toward the earth. So even if we are rooted in heaven, we still have to grow toward the earth—nobody asks if we want to.

When life does not make sense, it is very hard to stay involved. It is very hard to keep doing something that does not make sense. There was a temptation to enter the Cathedral, it is true. But a broken promise would have meant I had let the Divine down. Clearly the Divine has guided every single step of my life up to this point, and will do so in the future. I must keep my commitment.

29

Journey to the Light

*I*AM NOT SURE if you can *develop* an intense
desire for the Light. Often we cannot even develop a love affair with another person, and a
love affair with the Divine is much more difficult
to attain to. Through our experiences in life we have to
reach the point of intensely wanting to know, wanting
to understand, and wanting to move on. Think how
much more difficult it is for premature babies to survive than babies delivered when their time is due.
Each of us has to go through the process of growing to
maturity.

The following dream was an inspiration, a dream
that needed little interpretation or commentary. One

thing it made clear is that the spiritual journey takes a long time. We have to consider that even a temple or cathedral is often not completed in the same century it was started. In the same way the Cathedral of Consciousness also takes time to complete. Inspiration can be a sustaining energy, but it does not mean you can lessen your efforts.

Whatever we gain by our own efforts to come closer to the Divine is never lost. And whenever we do make contact, we can never forget. The memory is too overpowering. The memory is too sweet. You want it again, so you pull yourself together and say, "I will give it another try," until you finally get there. It is just like exercising muscles, except in this case, it is exercising the mind to overcome obstacles and resistance. People often find it difficult to attain to a spiritual state because they resist. Resisting the Divine is also the source of depressions and negative moods. You know that the Divine is standing behind the door, but you do not want to open it. You wonder fearfully, "What is She going to ask?" "What is He going to demand?" And yet you want . . . and you don't want, you want and you don't want. Because you cannot make up your mind, you resist. Nobody holds you back except yourself.

In the dream I am presented with a choice: I can continue to go through the swamp and probably eventually sink into it, disappear, and find my spiritual death; or I can enter the stream, which has a more solid base. The swamp to me is life without purpose. Some people say they want spiritual life but they still want to keep their business interests, their family interests, and their control over future plans; then they get lost in the morass of life itself. But walking against the current demands tremendous effort. Living opposed to the normal concepts of life, which I have done, does require effort. Stones in the water are certainly not a soft cushion or carpet for the feet. So if anyone wants to find out what it really means to live a spiritual life, they have to be prepared to go through the trials.

It is not a comfortable journey.

Journey to the Light

I am crossing some marshlands, jumping from one wooden board to another with a small bundle of my possessions. (Someone must have placed the planks here and there along the way.) Then I see a small stream with stones on the bottom, which looks like a firmer, safer base than the marshy morass. Although I have never walked with bare feet very much, I take off my shoes and enter the stream. The water is knee deep and the ground proves to be firm, as I had hoped. But I realize that it is not so easy to walk against the water.

I know that my destination is another shore, and that there will be a house there, and that I am expected. The stream gradually becomes a river, and then widens almost to the size of an ocean so vast that the opposite shore is now invisible. But I just know I have to make it there. I have no choice. I tie my bundle to the top of my head and decide to swim—it is the only solution, since the water has become too deep to walk through. I am not a very good swimmer so I think things through first. I decide to breathe regularly, take slow, big strokes, and not to hurry, in order to maintain my strength to the very last moment. I am convinced that I will be able to make it.

For some time I can see a dim little light, which I believe comes from "that" house. But then it, too, disappears and I start to get worried about how I will stay on course. Then I become aware that the water has a warm stream, which seems to go straight ahead. I try to keep to this warmer stream. My feet seem especially sensitive to recognizing the difference in temperature while swimming.

Finally I reach the shore. Again I see the little light more clearly, but I am surprised that it still seems far away. At first I think of taking a rest, but then, looking again at the light, I decide to keep going and get it over with. Moving ahead seems a little easier now. The field between the shore and the house is a soft kind of grass. But still I cannot seem to cover the ground as quickly as I thought, and the distance seems greater than I had anticipated.

At last I reach the house, only to face one more obstacle—there is no door. Yet I know, very definitely, that I am at the right place. Above the ground are large windows. I see there is no other way in but to climb up. Even though I do not like climbing and it looks as if it will be difficult to hold on and balance myself, there is no choice. I walk around the house. Light floods from the windows and almost blinds me, but I know I have to climb up anyway. I cannot wait here forever, so near my goal.

The building is solid stone. I get a grip with just my fingertips and toes, and inch my way up. It is a terrible struggle. At the last moment, just when I think I can't make it, my hand reaches the windowsill, and the window opens from the inside. I am pulled into the room. When I am inside I look at my helper with great relief, knowing that now it is all over!

The helper is a being of such indescribable beauty that I fall to the floor and just stare. That is all I feel capable of.

This wonderful being—I do not know if it is an angel or a bodhisattva—beaming with great joy, says, "All people must come sooner or later. All must find their way."

The helper directs me to look out the window. I see many, many little dots of light like glow-worms or fireflies.

I say, "But when I was swimming and walking here, I did not see any of these. I would have been happy if I had. It was very dark, and I was absolutely alone."

"They feel alone, too. Utterly alone. It cannot be otherwise. But would you like to help them, now that you are here?"

"Me? I can't do anything!"

"You can say a prayer, can you not?"

I agree. When I look out the window, suddenly I feel again the strain and anxiety I had felt along the way, and a wave of compassion overcomes me.

"Dear Lord, let none get lost," is all I can manage. The prayer seems to come from my heart rather than from my mouth. In fact I am aware of how insufficient, meaningless, and empty words are—how sentimental.

When this servant of the Light motions me to turn around and sit down, I see that what had appeared to be a small house is really an enormous palace, extraordinarily beautiful and bright. More light floods through a sliding door, and then I hear indescribable music, unlike anything I have ever heard, like big choirs, from nowhere and everywhere. This music has a tremendous impact on me. This "Choir of Souls," I call it for lack of words, touches me to the core and I feel over-awed.

The central thought in the dream is that I *must* reach my destination. I *must* arrive at Cosmic Consciousness, at the Divine, however dim or vague my ideas about it. "I just must" has so far truly kept me going, and the dream shows me it will continue to do so until all is done. The one thing that stays permanent throughout is my attraction to the Light. It is the propelling force that keeps me moving on. I never consider giving up.

Crossing the stream would have been very easy, but continuing right to the end—from the very narrow stream to the point where the river merges into the ocean, and then crossing to "the other shore"—that is a different challenge. The warm stream on the feet told me that as long as I stay in touch with my enthusiasm and intuition, I will keep going in the right direction. But the moment I experiment or try something easier, I may end up off course; I may literally cool off and let the direction go.

I am being led into the room where the voices of many are heard chanting the divine glories. In the scriptures it says some will be carried to the heavens to do just that. Others are like bodhisattvas, who offer to come back to help further the divine work.

This dream showed me that the higher mind is quite capable of perceiving other dimensions, but that the message has to be passed along in a way that the ordinary mind can understand, otherwise the meaning will remain concealed. Here was the map for my journey to the Light.

The dream's message is clear: if you persist you will get there.

30

Conclusion

*T*HE INDEPENDENCE you have always wanted is now at your fingertips. By working with your dreams, you can learn to trust and depend on your own inner processes and free yourself from the judgments of others. Often our many different life experiences create a strong sense of doubt—about ourselves and our potential, about the existence of another reality, about the existence of the Divine. These kinds of doubts are difficult to overcome. But how can you doubt dreams, which arise from your own mind? And even if you do doubt the truth of your dreams, they nevertheless can challenge you to test their truths, until eventually you will know.

My suggestion is that you try to get in touch with the inner Light in yourself through dreams. Shift your focus away from your personality—your physical, emotional, and mental existence—and come to really know this other part. Any teacher can only provide inspiration. My own Guru was very demanding, but he could do only so much. Then it was up to me. I had to depend on the guidance from within.

No one can give us what our own inner Guru can. But remember, this Guru is like any other teacher. It can suggest what you should do and point out the direction, but *you* have to do it. You have a great deal of freedom, if you will take the responsibility to handle that freedom. We often want to do things "our way," and with dreams we are given that chance, but we have to take the opportunity. How will you put your dreams into action?

We live in a tangible, physical world, which has its own reality, and we live in a mental world, a world of the unseen. When we go beyond the world of our ordinary stream of thoughts, we come into a world of consciousness. Once you know that this other reality exists—even if you touch it only once—it creates a desire to return again. I hope this book has shown you that dreams can be the vehicle which can take you there.

But do not believe a word I am saying.
Find out for yourself.

~

Suggested Reading

*Asterisked selections are noted in the text.

*The Bible. King James Version. With its many references to dreams and visions throughout, the Bible illustrates the Jewish and Christian understanding of dreams as divine messages.

*BROOK, STEPHEN. *The Oxford Book of Dreams.* Oxford: Oxford University Press, 1983. A thematic overview of dreams of historic and literary figures.

BRUCE, ROBERT D. *Lacandon Dream Symbolism.* Perugino, Mexico: Ediciones Euroamericanas Klaus Thiele, 1979. Dream symbols of the Lacandon Indians offer insights into Mayan culture and a perspective of the differences in dream symbolism between contemporary Western culture and that of an ancient civilization.

BRUNTON, PAUL. *The Wisdom of the Overself.* New York: Samuel Weiser, 1943. The spiritual value of sleep and dreams, the function of personality in evolution, development of intuition.

BULKELEY, KELLY. *The Wilderness of Dreams.* New York: State University of New York Press, 1993. A cross-disciplinary study of the essentially religious meaning of dreams.

CAMPBELL, JOSEPH. *The Mythic Image*. Princeton: Princeton University Press, 1974. A large illustrated work bringing to life images and myths from East and West. Starts with "The World as Dream" and ends with "Waking."

_____, ed. *Myths, Dreams and Religion*. Dallas: Spring Publications, 1988. A collection of lectures from the late 1960's, including works from Campbell, Alan Watts, Norman O. Brown, Ira Progroff. How dream and myth interface with religion, philosophy, and the arts.

*CAPRA, FRITJOF. *The Tao of Physics*. Boston: Shambhala Publications, 1975. An example of how Eastern symbolism comes alive in today's world of quantum physics.

CARTWRIGHT, R. and LAMBERG, L. *Crisis Dreaming*. New York: HarperCollins, 1992. Dreams as vehicles for assimilating major life changes.

CASTANEDA, CARLOS. *The Art of Dreaming*. New York: HarperCollins, 1993. A very different approach to dreams and levels of reality—that of the Yacqui sorcerers of Mexico. An investigative adventure.

*CHANG, GHARMA C. C. *Six Yogas of Naropa & Teachings on Mahamudra*. Ithaca, N.Y.: Snow Lion Publications, 1963. The teachings of the 11th century Indian Guru whose work contributed to Tibetan yoga practices. Particularly see "Instructions on the Dream Yoga" and "Instructions on the Light Yoga."

CLIFT, JEAN DALBY and CLIFT, WALLACE B. *Symbols of Transformation in Dreams*. New York: Crossroad, 1987. The symbolic language of dreams and transformational motifs from a Christian perspective.

COVITZ, JOEL. *Visions of the Night: A Study of Jewish Dream Interpretation*. Boston: Shambhala, 1990. An examination of historical Jewish methods of studying dreams and how this knowledge can be applied today.

COXHEAD, DAVID and HILLER, SUSAN. *Dreams:Visions of the Night*. New York: Avon Books, 1976. Weaving together dream and mythic images from many cultures with an intelligent text and quotations from a wealth of sources, this book is a tribute to the value of dreaming.

DAVID-NEEL, ALEXANDRA. *Initiations and Initiates in Tibet*. Fred Rothwell, trans. London: Rider and Co., 1958. Refer particularly to chapter on "Daily Spiritual Exercises" for instructions in sleeping postures, visualizations, and awareness in the dream state.

DE BECKER, RAYMOND. *The Understanding of Dreams*. Michael Heron, trans. New York: Hawthorn Books, 1968. A fascinating review of the "great religious dreams" (from Judaism, Christianity, Islam, Buddhism), the great political dreams, the great cultural dreams, and dreams in art and literature. Analyzes attitudes toward and interpretations of dreams throughout the ages and cultures.

DELANEY, GAYLE. *Living Your Dreams*. San Francisco: Harper & Row, 1979. Offers methods of "dream incubation" and "dream interviewing" to help understand dreams as problem-solvers.

DONIGER, WENDY and BULKELEY, KELLY. "Why Study Dreams? A Religious Studies Perspective." *Dreaming* (1993) vol.3, no.1:69-73. The authors suggest that a religious studies perspective of dreams can lead to the understanding of the complex cultural systems of the past and to insights into the spiritual nature of our dreams now.

DUNNE, JOHN W. *An Experiment With Time*. 3d ed. 1927. Reprint. London: Faber & Faber, 1958. Experiments with precognitive dreams lead the author to question the nature of time and the universe.

*EVANS-WENTZ, W. Y., ed. *Tibet's Great Yogi: Milarepa*. London: Oxford University Press, 1969. This account of a yogi who attained enlightenment in one lifetime also illustrates the significance of dreams and symbolism in spiritual development.

_____.*Tibetan Book of the Dead*. Oxford: Oxford University Press, 1957. Compares the after-death state (the Bardo) to a prolonged dreamlike state, intimating the necessity of directing the mind to the Clear Light in dreams as a preparation for death.

GARRISON, OMAR V. *Tantra: The Yoga of Sex*. New York: Julian Press, 1964. Refer especially to the chapter entitled, "Yoga of the Dream State."

GASKELL, G. A. *Dictionary of all Scriptures and Myths*. New York: Julian Press, 1960. Useful for gaining insight into the metaphorical language underlying myths and symbols.

GENDLIN, EUGENE. *Let Your Body Interpret Your Dreams*. Wilmette, Ill.: Chiron, 1986. From the author of *Focusing*, an approach to interpreting dreams through body awareness.

*GUENTHER, HERBERT. *The Life and Teaching of Naropa*. Oxford: Oxford University Press, 1963. A biography of the influential teacher and yogi. Refer especially to the sections on "Dream" and "The Radiant Light."

HOBSON, J. ALLAN. *The Dreaming Brain*. New York: Basic Books, 1988. Dreams in relation to physiology.

HUME, R. E., transl. *The Thirteen Principal Upanishads*. Oxford: Oxford University Press, 1921, 1971. See especially the Brihad-Aranyaka Upanishad, the Chandogya Upanishad, the

Prasna Upanishad, and the Mandukya Upanishad for the Indian scriptural view of dreams and the four states of self.

JUNG, C. G. *Dreams.* Princeton: Princeton University Press, 1974. A compilation of Jung's writings on dreams.

_____. *Man and His Symbols.* Garden City, N.Y.: Doubleday, 1964. A richly illustrated exploration of the meaning of symbols, and an introduction to Jung's approach to dream analysis. Includes articles by himself as well as by his closest followers.

_____. *Memories, Dreams and Reflections.* New York: Pantheon Books, 1961. Jung's personal memoirs, including his own significant dreams.

KHEDKAR, DR. R.V. *The Dream Problem and Its Many Solutions In Search After Ultimate Truth (A Symposium).* Ram Narayan, ed. Delhi: Practical Medicine Publishers, 1922. Western and Eastern "solutions" to an intriguing problem about the nature of reality and dream.

KLUGER, RIVKAH SCHARF. *The Archetypal Significance of Gilgamesh: A Modern Ancient Hero.* Einsiedeln, Switzerland: Daimon Verlag, 1991. A Jungian interpretation of the four thousand year old classic epic of Gilgamesh, highlighting the importance of the dreams within the epic.

KRIPPNER, STANLEY, ed. *Dreamtime and Dreamwork: Decoding The Language of the Night.* Los Angeles: J. P. Tarcher, 1990. An anthology of contemporary authors' views on a wide range of aspects of dreaming.

LAYARD, JOHN. *The Lady of the Hare.* 1944. Reprint. Boston: Shambhala, 1988. An analyst describes the transformative process in an English village woman as he works with her on the archetypal nature of her dreams. Layard extensively develops her key dream symbol, the hare, through cross-cultural mythology.

MACKENZIE, NORMAN. *Dreams and Dreaming.* New York: Vanguard Press, 1965. A profusely illustrated textbook of dreams providing a historical overview, an investigation of the major psychological theories, and some of the early scientific research.

*MAETERLINCK, MAURICE. *The Life of the Bee.* 1901. Reprint. Alfred Sutro, trans. New York: The New American Library, 1954. A Nobel Prize-winning author's work about life in the hive. Contained a message about my dream of the Queen of the Bees.

MAHONEY, MARIA. *The Meaning in Dreams and Dreaming: The Jungian Viewpoint.* Secaucus, N.J.: Citadel Press, 1966. A clear introduction to the Jungian approach to dreams, with guidelines on and examples of how to work with a variety of dreams.

*MAIMONIDES, MOSES. *Guide of the Perplexed. Book I.* Friedlander, trans. New York: Dover, 1956. Twelfth century Jewish philosopher outlines his scriptural interpretations. Especially note the section on the "Twelve Degrees of Prophecy," relating to Biblical dreams and visions.

MILLER, PATRICIA COX. *Dreams In Late Antiquity: Studies In the Imagination of a Culture.* Princeton: Princeton University Press, 1994. Dreams in the Graeco-Roman culture and their application to ethical, psychological, and spiritual problem-solving.

MISHRA, UMESHA. "Dream Theory in Indian Thought." *Allahabad University Studies.* (1929) 5:269-321. A fairly obtuse overview of the various streams of Indian thought on dreams, but useful for scriptural references.

MOFFAT, A. and KRAMER, M., eds.*The Functions of Dreaming*. New York: State University of New York Press, 1993. Scholarly essays and contemporary scientific and neurological research on dreaming.

MOTHER, THE. *Health and Healing in Yoga: Selections from the Writings and Talks of The Mother*. Pondicherry, India: Sri Aurobindo Ashram Trust, 1979. See especially "Rest, Sleep, and Dreams" for advice from a fairly contemporary woman teacher.

MULLER, MAX, ed. *Sacred Books of the East*. 1894. Reprint. Delhi: Motilal Banarsidass, 1965.
　　—vol.1. *The Upanishads*. See especially the Khandogya Upanishad, which claims that both dreams and waking life are relatively unreal, yet each can "have a true element in them" of the spiritual nature.
　　—vol. 3. *The Texts of Confucianism*. See "The Shih King," for an example of how the "Diviner of Dreams" interpreted them.
　　—vol. 36. *The Questions of King Milinda Part II*. In the section called the 75th Dilemma, "Dreams and Sleep," the sage Nagasena advises the seeker, King Milinda, that the only true dreams are of "prognostication," or the "divine intention."
　　—vol. 38. *Vedanta-Sutras*. "II Adhyaya" "Even in the state of dream the instruments of the Self are not altogether at rest."
　　—vol. 48. *Vedanta-Sutras*. "III Adhyaya". In contrast to Freud's view that dreams are wish-fulfillment, this sutra suggests that if dreams were expressive only of one's own wishes, no one would have dreams of ill fortune. "Hence the creation which takes place in dreams can be the Lord's work only."

MUSES, C. A., ed. *Esoteric Teachings of The Tibetan Tantra*. Chang Chen Chi, trans. York Beach, Maine.: Samuel Weiser, 1961. See particularly the chapter, "The Practice of Dream Yoga."

NORBU, NAMKHAI. *Dream Yoga and the Practice of Natural Light.* M. Katz, ed. Ithaca, N.Y.: Snow Lion, 1992. An engaging book that shows the living tradition of Tibetan dream yoga practices through the experiences of one of its teachers. Clarifies the motivational difference between the yogic approach and what has come to be called "lucid dreaming" in the West.

O'FLAHERTY, WENDY DONIGER. *Dreams, Illusions, and Other Realities.* Chicago: University of Chicago Press, 1984. A challenge to common concepts of reality through accounts of dreams, myths, and the arts in Indian religions.

*RADHA, SWAMI SIVANANDA. *Divine Light Invocation.* 3d ed. Spokane, Wash.: Timeless Books, 1990. A complete introduction to a transformative tool for cultivating the imagination.

*_____. *From The Mating Dance To The Cosmic Dance.* Spokane, Wash.: Timeless Books, 1992. Practical guidance on how the pursuit of Higher Consciousness can be understood in the context of sex, love, and marriage. Elucidates the role of fantasy and the "Dream Lover."

*_____. *Guided Meditation.* Spokane, Wash.: Timeless Books. Audio cassette.

*_____. *Hatha Yoga: The Hidden Language.* Spokane, Wash.: Timeless Books, 1987. Explores the potential of discovering the personal and universal symbolism of Hatha Yoga postures and the interplay of body and mind through reflection.

*_____. *In the Company of the Wise.* Spokane, Wash.: Timeless Books, 1991. Meetings with many spiritual teachers of different traditions.

*_____. *Kundalini Yoga For The West.* Spokane, Wash.: Timeless Books, 1978. A complete system for the development of character, courage, and awareness as a foundation for the pursuit of Higher Consciousness.

*_____. *Mantras: Words of Power*: Rev. ed. Spokane, Wash.: Timeless Books, 1994. A complete guidebook to Mantras—powerful sound formulas used for directing the mind and cultivating devotion.

*_____. *Radha: Diary of a Woman's Search*. Spokane, Wash.: Timeless Books, 1981. The adventure of living with and learning from a Guru.

_____. *Relaxation*. Spokane, Wash.: Timeless Books. Audio cassette. The practice of relaxing the body, relaxing the mind, and opening to higher awareness.

*_____. *Symbolism in Daily Life*. Spokane, Wash.: Timeless Books. Audio cassette.

*_____. *The Body Garden*. Spokane, Wash.: Timeless Books. Audio cassette.

REED, HENRY. *Dream Solutions*. San Rafael, Calif.: New World Library, 1991. A four week dream journal of meditations and exercises based on the work of C. G. Jung and Edgar Cayce.

ROERICH, GEORGE N. *The Blue Annals*. Delhi: Motilal Banarsidass, 1949. A translation of a Tibetan historical record of doctrines and teachers originally compiled in 1478. Numerous references to dreams as inspiration and guidance scattered throughout.

RYBACK, D. SWEITZER, L. *Dreams That Come True*. New York: Ivy Books, 1988. A ten year study of precognitive dreams.

SANFORD, JOHN A. *Dreams and Healing*. Ramsey, N. J.: Paulist Press, 1978. An overview of the spiritual heritage of dreams and their ability to heal. Two case histories show the interconnection between life events and dreams.

SAVARY, LOUIS M.; BERNE, PATRICIA H.; and WILLIAMS, STREPHON KAPLAN. *Dreams and Spiritual Growth: A Christian Approach to Dreamwork.* Ramsey, N.J.: Paulist Press, 1984. Traces the history of dreams in the Christian tradition and provides many useful techniques for contemporary dreamwork.

SELIGSON, F. J. *Oriental Birth Dreams.* Elizabeth, N. J.: Hollym International Corp., 1989. Birth as a symbol in Eastern women's dreams, and dreams of significant and mythical births (as, for example, the birth of the Buddha).

SINHA, JADUNATH. *Indian Psychology.* Stanford: Kegan, Paul, Trench, Trubmer, 1934. See chapter entitled "Dreams" for a sampling of Indian religious and philosophic views on dreaming.

SIVANANDA, SWAMI. *Bliss Divine.* Rishikesh, India: Yoga Vedanta Forest Academy, 1964. See especially Section 16 for a succinct explanation of the various states of consciousness relating to dreams and waking, the role of the mind, and the silent witness beyond all mental activity.

_____. *Concentration and Meditation.* Rishikesh, India: Divine Life Society, 1955.

*_____, commentary. *Bhagavad Gita.* Durban: Sivananda Press, 1968.

STEIGER, BRAD. *American Indian Medicine Dream Book.* Atglen, Pa.: Schiffer Publishing, 1993. Dreams in relation to American Indian culture.

TAYLOR, JEREMY. *Dream Work: Techniques For Discovering The Creative Power in Dreams.* New York: Paulist Press, 1983. A very readable and instructive book on dreams and group work. Includes a chapter on"Lucid Dreaming and Dream Yoga." Thorough, annotated bibliography.

_____. *Where People Fly and Water Runs Uphill.* New York: Warner, 1992. Case histories of dreamwork for problem-solving and hints for personal and group practice.

TEDLOCK, BARBARA, ed. *Dreaming: Anthropological and Psychological Interpretations.* Santa Fe, N. Mex.: School of American Research Press, 1992. Cross-cultural anthropological study of dreams in Eastern and Western cultures.

THURSTON, MARK A. *How To Interpret Your Dreams: Practical Techniques Based on The Edgar Cayce Readings.* Virginia Beach, Va.: A.R.E. Press, 1978. Contains various useful techniques for understanding the meaning of dreams and provides an overview of the Cayce approach.

ULLMAN, MONTAGUE and ZIMMERMAN, NAN. *Working With Dreams.* Los Angeles: J. P. Tarcher, 1979. A practical approach to group dreamwork that affirms the authority of the individual dreamer.

ULLMAN, MONTAGUE and KRIPPNER, STANLEY. *Dream Telepathy: Experiments in Nocturnal ESP.* Baltimore: Penguin Books, 1974. Detailed descriptions of controlled experiments in dream telepathy that the authors conducted over many years. Readers are left to draw their own conclusions.

VASAVADA, A.U. *Tripura-Rahasya (Jnanakhanda): English Translation and a Comparative Study of the Process of Individuation.* Varanasi, India: Chowkhamba Sanskrit Series Office, 1965. Indian text in which a Guru spins out stories within stories and dreams within dreams to convey to his disciple the multi-layered nature of reality. In the second part of the book the author compares this Eastern approach to the Jungian view of individuation.

VAUGHAN-LEE, LLEWELLYN. *The Lover and the Serpent.* Longmead, England: Element Books, 1990. Dreams in relation to the Sufi tradition from an analytical perspective.

VON FRANZ, MARIE-LOUISE. *Dreams.* Boston: Shambhala Publications, 1991. One of Jung's closest disciples writes on the nature of dreams, on Jung's personal process, and on the meaning of some historical figures' dreams.

VON GRUNEMBAUM, G. E. and CAILLOIS, ROGER. *The Dream and Human Societies.* Berkeley: University of California Press, 1966. A collection of lectures that form a comparative study of dreams in different cultures, especially focusing on the Near East and Islam.

WAYMAN, ALEX. "Significance of Dreams in India and Tibet." *History of Religions.* (1967)7:1-12. A brief overview of Hindu, Buddhist, and Jain thought about the nature of dreams, their prophetic aspect, and different systems of classification.

WOODMAN, MARION. *Leaving My Father's House: A Journey to Conscious Femininity.* Boston: Shambhala Publications, 1993. A Jungian analyst helps three women work through their difficult experiences by using their waking and dreaming experiences and a myth about awakening the feminine within.

WOODS, RALPH L., ed. *The World of Dreams, An Anthology. The Mystery, Grandeur, Terror, Meaning and Psychology of Dreams, As Told By The World's Greatest Writers, Philosophers, Theologians, Historians, Scientists, Psychiatrists and Psychologists From Ancient Times to Today.* New York: Random House, 1947. An encyclopedic compendium of dream approaches from East to West.

Index

Lincoln, Abraham   110
listening   151, 209, 215,
 269, 289
 intuitively   281
 to the Higher Self   193
 to yourself   145
Lord's Prayer, the   221
love   196, 225, 227
 for the Divine   313
 human and Divine
  314-315

powers of the   108, 184
programming of the   221
the creator   178
the interpreter   78, 178
the weaver   181, 224
trickiness of the   181, 311
under intense pressure
 114
Mind Watch   186
mistakes   68, 90, 126,
 178, 288

Maeterlinck, Maurice   101
Maimonides, Moses   77
*Man Crouched in the Sewer
 Pipe*   92-93
Mantra   130, 263, 272,
 275, 299
 before sleep   266
 maintaining through the
  night   267
 receiving, in dream   152
Maya   249
meditation   181, 194
memory   21, 184, 202,
 203, 316
 echo of experience   316
 training the   185
mind   7
 and consciousness   197
 barriers of the   200, 203
 control of   2
 creativity of the   224, 248
 directing the   241
 emptying, of residue   201
 feeding the   125, 179, 226
 hidden place of the   270
 in constant movement   183
 map of the   2

Names on the Board   106
nightmares   89-94
 children's   94
 of being attacked   92
 of being chased   92
 overcoming   89, 90, 93
Not Good For You!   124

observation   109, 185, 206
 of a flower   245
 of the mind   265
observer, the   181
oneness   127, 196

perception   7, 178, 198,
 203, 218, 219, 244
 intuitive   109, 136, 231,
  264, 281
personality aspects   86, 92,
 143, 191, 195, 270,
 301, 311
Pope   195, 197, 315
prayer   263, 266, 272,
 276, 289

About the Author

For more than 35 years Swami Sivananda Radha has expressed the most profound teachings of the East in simple, clear and straightforward language, making them more accessible to those who wish to attain to Higher Consciousness. Author of many classic books on Eastern philosophy, she has, through her experience with yoga, gained a true understanding of Eastern symbolism and an ability to communicate this knowledge to the Western seeker.

She has lectured all over North America and internationally at universities, colleges, churches, and psychological institutes, and is one of the most widely-known spiritual teachers today. Translations of her books are available in many languages, including French, Spanish, Italian, German, and Dutch.

Classes and Workshops

Workshops and classes based on Swami Radha's teachings are available from her ashram in Canada—Yasodhara Ashram—and at affiliated centers, called Radha Houses, located in urban communities internationally.

For further information on programs offered by Yasodhara Ashram or the Radha Houses (including a vacation and yoga retreat center in Mérida, Mexico) write: The Program Secretary, Yasodhara Ashram, PO Box 9RD, Kootenay Bay, BC, Canada V0B 1X0.

Further Inquiries

To obtain a free catalogue of all books, audio cassettes, and video tapes by Swami Sivananda Radha please write: Timeless Books, PO Box 3543RD, Spokane, WA 99220.